Famous
Last Words

"I can die now, I've lived twice."
Edith Piaf

"Death itself isn't dreadful, but hanging seems an awkward way of entering the adventure."
Gerald Chapman

"I've just read that I am dead. Don't forget to delete me from your list of subscribers."
Rudyard Kipling

"If this is dying, then I don't think much of it." – Lytton Strachey

"Dying is a very dull, dreary affair. And my advice to you is to have nothing whatever to do with it."
Somerset Maugham

"Go on, get out. Last words are for fools who haven't said enough."
Karl Marx

"Either that wallpaper goes, or I do."
Oscar Wilde

"Too late for fruit, too soon for flowers."
Walter de la Mare

"Damn it ...Don't you dare ask God to help me."
Joan Crawford

Famous Last Words

The Ultimate Collection of Finales and Farewells

Laura Ward

PRC

Produced in 2004 by
PRC Publishing Limited
The Chrysalis Building
Bramley Road, London W10 6SP

An imprint of **Chrysalis** Books Group plc

This edition published in 2004
Distributed in the U.S. and Canada by:
Sterling Publishing Co., Inc.
387 Park Avenue South
New York, NY 10016

ISBN 1 85648 708 3

Printed and bound in Malaysia

Contents

Introduction

Die, my dear doctor? That's the last thing I shall do.

Samuel Palmerston, British Prime Minister

Never a truer word spoken. Death does indeed come to us all, and it is literally the last thing we all will do—not for nothing is it called the Great Leveller. The high and mighty, the rich and famous, the great and the good, the best and the worst of the human race—mere mortals, one and all—each and every one of us will surely turn to dust.

Not that Lord Palmerston meant it quite like that—his was a defiant stance, announcing his intention to live life to the full; the hour of his demise was not, as far as he was concerned, yet nigh. But to no avail. Saints or sinners, do-gooders or ne'er do wells; artists, adventurers, aristocrats; scribblers, scientists, soldiers; pen-pushers, preachers, prime ministers, presidents—

immortality is not an option, and "immunity" against a Certain End cannot be secured. To quote Benjamin Franklin, "Nothing is certain except death and taxes;" a sentiment echoed thirty years afterward by Eliza Bonaparte, sister of the defeated French emperor, when she was told that nothing was certain except death. "Except taxes" was her reply.

On the face of it, then, the dying words and significant final utterances of the famous (and not so famous) might not seem to be the most cheery of subjects to investigate. Nonetheless, I'll bet, if you're reading this, that you already know of a few famous last quips—perhaps the oft-quoted Douglas Fairbanks Sr. declaring, "I've never felt better" (surely, asking for trouble?); or the English author J. M. Barrie muttering, "I can't sleep." (Then doing just that— well and good.) Or, Julius Caesar gasping, "Et tu, Brute?" as the Roman Emperor received the fatal dagger blows; or John Sedgwick riposting, "Nonsense, they couldn't hit an elephant at this dist—" as he inadvisably put his head above the parapet during the Battle of the Wilderness.

And perhaps you too have a certain secret fascination with final farewells and dying declarations, and other such phrases of finality. I confess that I have a foolish—possibly romantic—notion that a person's departing sentence, however brief, can tell us something about the life that preceded it, and perhaps even throw fresh light on that individual. Of course, the "famous last word" can just as easily be a prosaic final utterance or request, which is perhaps just as interesting as the more high-minded declarations. "Water" was the express desire of President Ulysses Simpson Grant as he lay on his deathbed. Which only goes to underline the common thread of humanity that binds us all.

However, all too often in the course of my research I would often come across an intriguing record of some such final utterance, fond adieu, or exclamation upon extirpation, then find myself wanting to know more. Why did Charles Dickens shout "On the ground!" or "Wild Bill" Hickok declare: "The old duffer—he broke me on the hand!" (Read on to find out!) With this in mind, I have attempted, where I felt entries cried out for it, to provide a context for many of the famous last words that have found their way into this book. And, particularly where historical figures are concerned—and about whom there is a wealth of contradictory information—to give some further elucidation.

Occasionally, digging deeper, I discovered different pieces of the same puzzle—a dying phrase or significant final utterance that could be counterbalanced with, say, a will, an epitaph, or an obituary, or other such "after-the-event" comment. This proved especially satisfying, painting as it does a broader picture. Similarly, stumbling across a note, diary entry, telegram, or letter which, while not written from a deathbed—or indeed anywhere near one—turns out, thanks to a cruel twist of fate, to be a "famous last word." The latter thereby becomes a form of farewell, an unintentional finality.

Then, speaking of unintentional finalities, there are the remarks that acquire a rich significance after the event—and, with the benefit of hindsight, seem almost to be inviting trouble. Take, for example, John F. Kennedy saying before his trip to Dallas, "If someone is going to kill me, they will kill me." And then the wife of the governor of Texas, to J. F. K. on his arrival in that city: "Well, Mr President, you can't say that the people of Dallas haven't given you a nice welcome." History cloaks such phrases in a deep layer of irony.

Irony, wisdom after the event, the benefit of 20/20 hindsight— all these different words refer to the same phenomenon. Which brings me neatly to the latter part of this book—those everyday "famous last words," in the sense of the muttered cliché; that is, you just wait and see, you'll be proved wrong. Or, more often, don't tempt fate. I have a long experience of this. Take the vacation where the hire car is struggling up a 45 degree incline, and starts to slide back—"Oh well, at least the handbrake works" says its nonchalant driver. Famous last words. Or, "This hike is only a short one," as a certain relative (who shall remain nameless but who should easily recognize himself) famously declares—then a perilous, slow descent from the snowy mountain as darkness falls and hunger sets in.

The list of silly examples could go on. But more interesting are the "biggies"—confident or universal assertions that later fall flat, predictions that turn out to be plain wrong. *The Brooklyn Daily Eagle* famously made such predictions as a new century—the twentieth century—dawned ("nobody who is anybody a hundred years hence but will have his automobile and his air yacht"). It is entertaining and illuminating to extract such nuggets from the past. For example, cannabis is highly effective as a cough medicine; submarines will simply sink (but the *Titanic* will never sink); tanks are of little use as weapons of war; women will never have the vote (and, according to Queen Victoria, should certainly not aspire to); Darwin is a nincompoop and the theory of evolution is mere stuff and nonsense ("I laughed till my sides were sore," was one response).

However, even better than such phrases, which the harsh light of history proves to be wrong, are the classic clangers from the mouths of those who must later wish they'd never spoken. For such individuals, a short span of time suffices to prove them so wrong. In this vein, one of my personal favorites is the comment by a poor missionary, the Reverend Thomas Baker, who declared in the nineteenth century that "Fijians are not lovers of human flesh." He was eaten shortly after by those very people he had sought to convert. On a lighter note, we find a young Rolling Stone by the name of Mick Jagger boasting "I'd rather be dead than singing *Satisfaction* when I'm 45." And Johnnie Cochran, of the O. J. Simpson murder trial, saying "The case is a loser." (It makes you wonder whether we should always hedge our bets, and avoid any declaration of absolute certainty.) And the higher they climb, the farther they have to fall. Take Richard Nixon in 1973 declaring, "I've got what it takes to stay." Or Gerald R. Ford saying "We have the momentum now, and I just know we are going to win" days before losing the 1976 presidential election. Or a famously blooper-prone Prince Philip, H. R. H. Duke of Edinburgh, during World War II complaining, "This is a dull war. There is no shooting." Or George H. W. Bush with the doomed, "Read my lips: No New Taxes" promise.

In sum, this volume offers up a compendium of finality in all its shades, from dying declarations, to dying of embarrassment, to plain dead wrong. Perhaps part of the fascination with the bons mots and famous last words that constitute the first, and undoubtedly the most important, of these categories is rooted in the reality that each one of us secretly wonders how he or she will work through their own final moments on this earth. After all, as the science writer Isaac Asimov once put it, "Life is pleasant. Death is peaceful. It's the transition that's troublesome."

This "transition" (and what a marvellous euphemism that is) comes in a variety of guises. The "mode," as the spy John André referred to it before his execution, might take the form of a welcome release, perhaps after a prolonged illness and much physical or mental suffering, or be a quiet slipping away after a life lived to its full measure of "three score years and ten." On the other side of the coin, there is the life full of promise that is cut short in its prime, from illness, perhaps, or scythed down in a field of action (military or otherwise). Almost every death leaves trauma or sadness in its wake—a family sundered, friends left bereft, even a nation in mourning. Yet the very subject is one many people spend much of their lives trying to avoid. Indeed, Samuel Johnson said, "The whole of life is but keeping away the thoughts of it." The Ancients, on the other hand, thought that the contemplation of the final reckoning was the best route to living a full and fruitful life. And many of the famous last words contained between these covers inject a note of light and cheer into what might otherwise be darkness.

Laura Ward

Final Quotations—
Literary Figures

Dying is a very dull, dreary affair. And my advice to you is to have nothing
whatever to do with it.

> *Somerset Maugham (d. 1965),*
> *to Robin Maugham, on his deathbed*

I've had eighteen straight whiskies, I think that's the record.

> *Dylan Thomas (d. 1953)—so saying, the Welsh poet exited*
> *from the White Horse Tavern in Greenwich Village to walk*
> *back to Chelsea Hotel, where he dropped dead*

Those damned doctors have drenched me so that I can scarcely stand. I want to
sleep now. Shall I sue for mercy? Come, come, no weakness. Let me be a man
to the last.

> *Lord Byron (d. 1824), English Romantic poet—"mad, bad, and*
> *dangerous to know"—and incorrigible womanizer. He died of*
> *fever, aged 36, while fighting in support of the Greeks*

More light! More light!

Johann Wolfgang von Goethe (d. 1832)—
last words of the German author, most famous for
the novella entitled The Sorrows of Young Werther

Is this a time to be making enemies?

Voltaire, French Enlightenment writer and philosopher,
when exhorted on his deathbed in 1778 if not to receive
the last sacrament, then at least to repudiate the devil.
He was denied a Christian burial as a consequence

Take me, for I come to Thee.

John Bunyon (d. 1688), English writer
and author of Pilgrim's Progress

Go away. I'm all right.

H.G. Wells (d. 1946), English writer. He was far from all right; ten
minutes later he was dead. He was speaking to his nurse, whom
he had summoned but then decided he did not need help after all

I have a strange pain in my head.

Hours before his death, the writer Robert Louis Stevenson
(d. 1894) was thus complaining to his wife.
He fell back unconscious, and died

God, I'm bored.

St. John Philby (d. 1905), Arabist

It's all been very interesting.

Lady Mary Wortley Montagu (d. 1762), writer,
early feminist, and socialite. And famous for
introducing the smallpox inoculation in England

Lord, help my poor soul.

Edgar Allan Poe (d. 1849), American poet and short-story writer

I can't sleep.

James M. Barrie (d. 1937), English author and creator of Peter Pan

Put that bloody cigarette out!

H. H. Munro ("Saki"), English storywriter, just before he was shot
by a sniper near Beaumont-Hamel, November 14, 1916

I knew it. I knew it! Born in a hotel room—and goddamit—dying in a hotel room.

Eugene O'Neill (d. 1953), American dramatist,
staring feverishly around his room at the Shelton Hotel,
Boston, before sinking into unconsciousness

I don't know. I don't know!

Pierre Abelard (d. 1142), French philosopher,
theologian, and teacher

Mind your own business!

> *Wyndham Lewis (d. 1957), British writer, when asked about the*
> *state of his bowels while languishing on his deathbed*

Will it be an interesting experience? Will I find out what lies behind the barrier?
  Why does it take so long to come?

> *Graham Greene (d. 1991), British novelist. His final questions—*
> *appropriate ones for a writer obsessed with sin and religion—*
> *were addressed to Yvonne Cloetta, his loyal companion*

In spite of it all, I am going to sleep.

> *Thomas B. Aldrich (d. 1907), poet and novelist*

Keep the rats away now that I am all greased up.

> *Pietro Aretino (d. 1557), Italian Renaissance dramatist, after*
> *having been anointed with Holy Oil during the Last Rites*

What's the news?

> *Clarence Walker Barron (d. 1928), publisher of the* Wall Street Journal

No. Thanks for everything.

> *Max Beerbohm (d. 1956), English caricaturist and*
> *critic, asked whether he had had a good sleep*

I am about the extent of a tenth of a gnat's eyebrow better.

Joel Chandler (d. 1908), American writer, when asked
how he was feeling—shortly after which he expired

Hullo.

Rupert Brooke (d. 1915), British poet, addressing
Denis Browne, who was to be his last visitor.
Brooke was dying of blood poisoning

Oh, I am not going to die, am I? He will not separate us, we have been so happy!

Charlotte Brontë (d. 1855), English novelist
(author of Jane Eyre*), spoken to her husband of*
only nine months, Reverend Arthur Nicholls

If you will send for a doctor, I will see him now.

Emily Brontë (d. 1848), author of Wuthering Heights. *The request*
came too late and she died young, as did her two sisters,
Charlotte and Anne, and her brother Patrick Branwell

Oh Lord! Forgive the errata!

Andrew Bradford (d. 1742), publisher of the American
Weekly Mercury, *the first newspaper in Philadelphia*

I can't hear very well. And there's a mist in front of my eyes. But it will go away,
won't it? Don't forget to open the window tomorrow.

> *Boris Pasternak (d. 1960), Russian writer and author of* Dr Zhivago. *These
> words, spoken on the night of his death, were to his wife Zinaida, but it
> seems he never stopped loving Olga Ivinskaya, the model for Lara in the
> book. His very last words were "Why am I hemorrhaging?" His wife
> reassured him that it was because of his pneumonia*

Beautiful.

> *Elizabeth Barrett Browning (d. 1861), when asked how she was feeling*

Have you brought the chequebook, Alfred?

> *Samuel Butler (d. 1902), English writer
> (author of* Erewhon *and* The Way of All Flesh*)*

That is surprising, since I have been practicing all night.

> *John Philpot Curran (d. 1817), Irish author and wit, to his doctor
> who had commented that he was coughing "with more difficulty"*

No. (And supposing you were?)

> *Robert Charles Benchley (d. 1945), American writer
> and humorist. He jotted the words down next to the
> title of an essay he was reading entitled "Am I thinking?"*

I shall have to ask leave to desist, when I am interrupted by so great an
experiment as dying.

> *Sir William Davenant (d. 1668), English playwright and*
> *poet laureate under the English King Charles II—he had put*
> *aside a poem on which he was working. Davenant was also,*
> *possibly, the illegitimate son of William Shakespeare*

Quick, Puss, chloroform—ether—or I am a dead man.

> *Sir Richard Burton (d. 1890), writer and translator of the*
> Arabian Nights, *addressing his wife Isabel by her pet name*

There, I have done! Oh, what triumphant truth!

> *Timothy Dwight (d. 1817), American author,*
> *as he finished his last manuscript*

Very weak. Rail to La Encina and Alicante.

> *Edward A. Freeman (d. 1892), historian, in his final diary entry*

I am very ill. Send for Zimmermann. In fact, I think I'll die today.

> *Ludwig Holty (d. 1776), German poet*

I am making my last effort to return that which is divine in me to that which is
divine in the Universe.

> *Plotinus (d. 270 BC), neoplatonic philosopher,*
> *in suitably philosophical frame of mind*

Everything is atoned for.

August Strindberg (d. 1912), Swedish dramatist

I am dying, sir, of one hundred good symptoms.

Alexander Pope (d. 1744), English poet and man of letters

He said he was dying of fast women, slow horses, crooked cards, and straight whiskey.

Kenneth Rexroth, American poet, recalling his father's dying words

Now it has come.

Laurence Sterne (d. 1768), English author

It is no use fighting death any more.

J. M. Synge (d. 1909), Irish dramatist

This is not my home.

Ludovico Ariosto (d. 1533), Italian poet

We shall go out together.

Marie Bashkirtseff (d. 1884), Russian diarist, watching the candle by her bedside

Whose house is this? What street is this? Would you like to see Miss Fairchild?

> *W. C. Bryant (d. 1878), American poet. He had tripped*
> *and hit his head on the sidewalk, the effect of which had*
> *disoriented him. Miss Fairchild was his niece*

When you come to the hedge that we must all go over, it isn't so bad. You feel sleepy, you don't care. Just a little dreamy anxiety, which world you're really in, that's all.

> *Stephen Crane (d. 1900), American author*

Turn up the lights. I don't want to go home in the dark.

> *O. Henry, nom de plume of William Sidney Porter*
> *(d. 1910), American short-story writer*

Here lies one whose name was written in hot water.

> *Robbie Ross (d. 1918), companion of Oscar Wilde,*
> *punning on the inscription on Keats' grave—*
> *"Here lies one whose name was writ on water"*

Severn, lift me up, for I am dying. I shall die easy. Don't be frightened. Be firm and thank God it has come.

> *John Keats (d. 1821), English Romantic poet, who died of tuberculosis at the*
> *age of 25. His words were to his friend Joseph Severn, in their lodgings in*
> *Piazza di Spagna in Rome—now the Keats–Shelley Memorial house*

The truth... I care a great deal... how they...

Nikolai Tolstoy (d. 1910), Russian novelist

Death, the only immortal, who treats us all alike, whose peace and whose
refuge are for all. The soiled and the pure, the rich and the poor, the loved and
the unloved.

Deathbed memorandum of Mark Twain (d. 1910), American
author and humorist, born Samuel L. Clemens

Here, veteran—if you think it right, strike.

Marcus Tullius Cicero (d. 43 BC), Roman writer,
to the soldier who killed him

I see the black light!

Victor Hugo (d. 1885), French poet, novelist, and committed
Republican. He was exiled when a monarchy of sorts was restored
in France following Napoleon Bonaparte's exile. He is also reported
as having said, more philosophically, "Here is the struggle between
day and night." ("C'est ici le combat du jour et de la nuit")

I have struggled with many difficulties. Some I have been able to overcome and
by some I have been overcome. I have made many mistakes but I love my
country and have labored for the youth of my country, and I trust no precept
of mine has taught any dear youth to sin.

Daniel Webster (d. 1843), American lexicographer,
after whom the famous dictionary is named

You crawl out of your mother's womb, you crawl across open country under fire,
  and drop into your grave.

> *Quentin Crisp (d. 1999)—toward the end of his own life, the wit, author,*
> *and gay activist presented a grim summation of life in general*

Sister, you're trying to keep me alive as an old curiosity, but I'm done, I'm
  finished, I'm going to die.

> *George Bernard Shaw (d. 1950), Irish playwright, man of letters*
> *and advocate of social reform (words spoken to his nurse)*

God bless...God damn.

> *James Thurber (d. 1961), American writer and humorist*

I am so happy, so happy.

> *Gerard Manley Hopkins (d. 1889), Jesuit priest and English poet,*
> *as he lay dying of typhoid after a life of self-denial*

No, it is not.

> *Oliver Goldsmith (d. 1774), author of* The Vicar of Wakefield, *in*
> *response to his physician's enquiry, "Is your mind at ease?"*

Give me! Give me! Come on, give me! The ladder! Quick, pass me the ladder!

> *Nikolai Gogol (d. 1852), Russian writer, already weak from fasting and*
> *now delirious on his deathbed, where he was administered a series of*
> *terrifying treatments by quack doctors. He was probably seeing the ladder*
> *which, he once wrote, extended down from heaven to save humanity*

Calmer and calmer.

> *Johann Friedrich Schiller (d. 1805), German dramatist,*
> *when asked how he was feeling*

It is some time since I drank champagne.

> *Anton Chekhov (d. 1904), Russian dramatist,*
> *as he lay dying of tuberculosis. (The doctors had,*
> *among other things, prescribed a glass of champagne)*

Bear witness that I have lived as a philosopher and die as a Christian.

> *Giovanni Jacopo Casanova (d. 1798), on the morning of his death—*
> *the lifelong womanizer turned philosopher in his dotage.*
> *The world's greatest lover is also supposed to have said (appropriately*
> *for him), "Life is a wench that one loves, to whom we allow any*
> *condition in the world, so long as she does not leave us"*

Too late for fruit, too soon for flowers.

> *Walter de la Mare (d. 1956), British Romantic poet,*
> *on being asked on his deathbed whether he would like*
> *some fruit or flowers. The answer was suitably elegiac*

On the contrary!

> *Henrik Ibsen (d. 1906), Norwegian dramatist. His nurse had*
> *remarked that he appeared to be a bit better; Ibsen did not think*
> *so ("Tvertimod!"); after this remark, he lapsed into unconsciousness*

I did not know that we had ever quarreled

*Henry David Thoreau (d. 1862), American writer and
aesthete, when asked whether he had made peace with his Maker.
During his final throes of tuberculosis, Thoreau muttered the words
"Moose... Indian" to his friend Ellery Channing. It was a beautiful spring
morning, and the words summed up the abiding preoccupations of his life*

God will pardon me. It is his profession.

*Heinrich Heine (d. 1856), German poet and writer,
on the eve of his death (probably from syphilis). The very
last words he uttered were, "Write! Write! Write! Paper! Pencil!"
He died unable to make feeble use of either instrument*

All right, then, I'll say it. Dante makes me sick.

*Lope Félix de Vega Carpio (d. 1635), Spanish dramatist,
on being told he was about to die*

Crito, I owe a cock to Asclepius; will you remember to pay him?

*Socrates, the Greek philosopher, on taking
the poison (d. 399 BC). It was customary to make an
offering to the gods upon recovery (Asclepius was the
god of medicine); with death being the final "recall,"
an offering would have been proper on his demise*

Either that wallpaper goes, or I do.

>*Last words of Oscar Wilde (d. 1900), Irish wit and dramatist, as he lay languishing in a drab Parisian hotel room, recorded in variant forms by R. H. Sherard,* Life of Oscar Wilde *(1906) and Richard Ellmann,* Oscar Wilde *(1988)*

So here it is at last, the distinguished thing.

>*Generally regarded as the dying words of Henry James (d. 1916), American born novelist. They gained credence through being recorded by Edith Wharton in* A Backward Glance *(1934), as reported to her by Lady Prothero, a confidante of James. James actually claimed to have heard the words when he had suffered his first stroke, on December 2, 1915*

Go on, get out. Last words are for fools who haven't said enough.

>*Karl Marx. As death approached, the creator of communism summoned his housekeeper, who urged him to tell her his last words so she could write them down for posterity. Marx didn't think so*

Going, going, where am I a-going? I'm sure, I know no more than the Man in the Moon.

>*"Frog" Walker, a contemporary of the poet Thomas Gray (author of* Elegy Written in a Country Churchyard*), in response to the nurse at his bedside who had cried, "Ah, poor gentleman, he is going!"*

Is it not meningitis?

> *Louisa May Alcott (d. 1888), author of* Little Women *and* Good Wives, *enquiring about the nature of the disease of which she was dying. She had typhoid, contracted while serving as a nurse in the American Civil War*

God bless you, my dear.

> *Last words of Samuel Johnson (d. 1784), English writer, as reported by James Boswell. They were addressed to a Miss Morris, who had called in to see Dr. Johnson. However, according to Sir John Hawkins, another biographer, Dr Johnson whispered "I am dying now" before expiring*

Stop—I turn home... I'm bored... I'm bored.

> *Gabriele d'Annunzio (d. 1938), Italian poet, dramatist, and soldier who lived to the age of 75. He was speaking to his chauffeur*

The hearse, the horse, the driver and—enough!

> *Luigi Pirandello (d. 1936), Italian dramatist*

Nothing, but death.

> *Jane Austen (d. 1817), English novelist, when asked by her sister Cassandra during her final illness—after several months of failing health—if there was anything she desired. She was only 42 when she died*

If Bianchon were here, he would save me.

> *Honoré de Balzac (d. 1850), French author of the*
> *epic series of novels,* La Comédie Humaine. *He was*
> *referring to his fictitious physician, Horace Bianchon*

It is well.

> *André Gide (d. 1951), French writer ("C'est bien")*

The issue is now clear. It is between light and darkness, and everyone must
choose his side.

> *G. K. Chesterton (d. 1936), British author and critic. Another*
> *version has him saying "hello my darling" to his wife, on one side*
> *of him, and "hello my dear" to his secretary, on the other*

Let me have my own fidgets.

> *Walter Bagehot (d. 1877), British economist, critic, and journalist;*
> *he was refusing help with rearranging his own pillows*

Take away those pillows; I shall need them no more.

> *Charles L. Dodgson, a.k.a. Lewis Carroll (d. 1898),*
> *Victorian scholar and author of* Alice in Wonderland

What possible harm could it do to me?

> *Denis Diderot (d. 1784), French Enlightenment author, to his wife*
> *who was remonstrating with him for eating an apricot ("Mais que*
> *Diable de mal veux-tu que cela me fasse?"—and then he died)*

God forbid that I should be sunk so low as to forget the offices of humanity.

Immanuel Kant (d. 1804), philosopher,
whose mind nonetheless failed him at the end

John, don't let the awkward squad fire over me.

Robert Burns (d. 1796), Scottish poet commemorated
annually in January's Burns Night celebrations. He also said to a
woman who offered to pull down the blind for him, "Oh! Let him
shine; he will not shine long for me"

Death twitches my ear. "Live," he says. "I am coming."

Virgil (d. 19 BC), author of the Aeneid, *which tells the*
story of Troy and the travels of Aeneas

Linen, doctor? You speak of linen? Do you know what linen is? The linen of the
peasant, of the worker? Linen is a great thing. I want to make a book of it.

Jules Michelet (d. 1874), French historian;
he was rambling when he spoke these words

So this is death. Well...

Thomas Carlyle (d. 1881), Victorian essayist and historian

It is now half-past nine. World, adieu!

Frederick Marryat (d. 1848), naval captain, adventure-story writer
and children's author (he wrote the Children of the New Forest*)*

On the ground!

> *Charles Dickens (d. 1870), who died of a stroke while still a
> relatively young man—his sister-in-law and friends were struggling
> to get him on to the sofa after he had collapsed at dinner*

By the Immortal God, I will not move.

> *Thomas Love Peacock (d. 1866), the Victorian writer who was
> burned to death while trying to save the books in his library*

God bless Captain Vere!

> *Herman Melville (d. 1891), whose most famous work was* Moby Dick. *But
> the words are quoted from another of his works,* Billy Budd

Then you really think I am dying? At last you think so. But I was right from
the first.

> *Dante Gabriel Rossetti (d. 1882), Pre-Raphaelite poet and painter—mainly
> of idealized portraits of women. He had all of his poems buried with
> his wife, Elizabeth Siddal. His sister was Christina Rossetti*

I love everybody. If ever I had an enemy, I should hope to meet and welcome
that enemy in heaven.

> *Christina Rossetti (d. 1894), poet and sister of Dante Gabriel Rossetti*

I must go in, the fog is rising.

> *Emily Dickinson (d. 1886), poetess; later, when
> offered a drink of water: "Oh, is that all it is?"*

I believe... I'm going to die. I love the rain. I want the feeling of it on my face.

Katherine Mansfield (d. 1923), New Zealand-born writer of short stories

Does nobody understand?

James Joyce (d. 1941), author of the (to some) impenetrable novel Ulysses

What is the answer?...In that case, what is the question?

Gertrude Stein (d. 1946), American writer

I think it is time for morphine.

D.H. Lawrence (d. 1930), English author of
Lady Chatterly's Lover *and* Women In Love

Well done. You are doing that very well, my boy.

Wilfred Owen (d. 1918), British poet, to one of the soldiers under
his command in World War I. He died in the trenches

I am about to take my last voyage, a great leap in the dark.

Thomas Hobbes (d. 1679), author of The Leviathan,
an early social treatise published in 1651

Sister! Sister!

Thomas de Quincey (d. 1859), English essayist and author of
Confessions of an English Opium-Eater. *The words were*
addressed, apparently, to a vision of Elizabeth, his dead sister

See in what peace a Christian can die.

> *Joseph Addison (d. 1719), English essayist, statesman, poet,*
> *and co-founder of the English magazine* The Spectator

Toodle-oo!

> *Last words of Allen Ginsberg (d. 1997), according to Ken Kesey*

Your ungrammatical style is putting me off them.

> *French poet François de Malherbes (d. 1628),*
> *forced on his deathbed to listen to an over-fulsome*
> *description of the heavenly paradise awaiting him*

Good enough; they'll be fine.

> *F. Scott Fitzgerald (d. 1940)—words spoken à propos of some*
> *Hershey chocolate bars moments before the writer collapsed in the*
> *Garden of Allah Hotel in Hollywood. He had been chatting*
> *to Sheilah Graham, saying "I'm going to Schwab's to get some*
> *ice cream." To which she had replied, "But you might miss the doctor.*
> *If it's something sweet you want, I've got some Hershey bars"*

Ah! A German and a genius! A prodigy—admit him!

> *Last words (allegedly) of Jonathan Swift (d. 1745), author of*
> Gulliver's Travels, *visited on his deathbed by the composer Handel*

If this is dying, then I don't think much of it.

> *Lytton Strachey (d. 1932), English writer and biographer*

Yes, my dear Robert, you are.

> *Marcel Proust (d. 1922), French author of the series of novels entitled*
> Remembrance of Things Past. *(His brother had asked if he was hurting him.)*
> *Earlier, the writer had been plagued by ghastly apparitions*

You are wonderful.

> *Sir Arthur Conan Doyle (d. 1930), creator of the fictional detective*
> *Sherlock Holmes—he was speaking to his wife Jean*

Heavily, like a big peasant woman.

> *Mme de Stael (d. 1817), French belletrist,*
> *when asked how she was going to sleep*

Tell them I have a great pain in the left side.

> *George Eliot (d. 1880),* nom de plume *of English novelist*
> *Mary Ann Evans, author of* Silas Marner *and* Daniel Deronda

Do you think it could have been the sausage?

> *Paul Claudel (d. 1955), French writer*

I go to seek the great Perhaps.

> *François Rabelais (d. 1553), French writer*
> *and creator of the fictional giant* Gargantua

Well, I must arrange my pillows for another night. When will this end?

Washington Irvine (d. 1859), American writer

I am going to the inevitable.

Philip Larkin (d. 1985), British poet, to his nurse on his deathbed

In Requiem—
Great Composers

Harmony.

Last word uttered by the composer Arnold Schoenberg who, obsessed with numerology, had predicted his own death (correctly, to the last minute) at 11.47 p.m. on Friday July 13, 1951 at the age of 76

Dear Gerda, I thank you for every day we have been together.

Ferruccio Busoni (d. 1924), Italian pianist and composer

Ah, that tastes nice. Thank you!

Johannes Brahms (d. 1897), German composer,
after sipping from a glass of wine

One thousand greetings to Balakirev.

Hector Berlioz (d. 1869), French composer

What's this?

Leonard Bernstein (d. 1990), composer

Hier, hier ist mein Ende.

> *Franz Schubert (d. 1828), Austrian composer, moments before*
> *his death. ("Here, here is my end.") Earlier, in his delirium,*
> *he had cried out, "This is not Beethoven lying here!"*

Mozart.

> *Gustav Mahler (d. 1911), Austrian composer. His thoughts were*
> *of a fellow composer, although his wife Alma was at his bedside*

Well, if it must be so.

> *Edvard Grieg (d. 1907), Norwegian composer*

Weary, very weary.

> *Felix Mendelssohn (d. 1847), French composer, asked how he was feeling*

Bad.

> *Hans Guido von Bülow (d. 1894), German conductor,*
> *when asked how he was feeling*

I am a pianist.

> *John Field (d. 1837), British pianist and composer.*
> *He had been asked, "Are you a Papist or a Calvinist?"*

I look like a Moor.

> *Maurice Ravel (d. 1937), French composer,*
> *looking at his bandaged head in the mirror*

I'm shot...it's over.

> *Anton Webern (d. 1945), Austrian composer,*
> *fatally wounded in a mysterious domestic shooting incident*

Too bad! Too bad! It's too late!

> *Ludwig van Beethoven (d. 1827); this version has him referring to*
> *the late arrival of the wine he had ordered—another has the deaf*
> *composer saying, "I shall hear in Heaven." Another says he sat up*
> *in bed, shook his fist (at what, who knows?) and fell back dead.*
> *Beethoven died after having been out during a violent hailstorm*

But I have so little time!

> *Alban Berg (d. 1935), Austrian composer (Wozzeck was his*
> *most famous piece), when asked by his wife to take it a little*
> *easier (he was working on a concerto during his final illness)*

I am in a cold sweat. Is it the sweat of death? How are you going to tell my
father?

> *Georges Bizet (d. 1875), French composer of* Carmen *fame*

Plus. ("No more.")

> *Frédéric Chopin (d. 1849), French composer. His idol*
> *was Mozart, and he begged for Mozart's* Requiem *to*
> *be played for him. Before the above final utterance, he said,*
> *"Maintenant, j'entre en agonie." ("Now is my final agony")*

If you wait a little, I shall be able to tell you from personal experience.

> *Christoph Gluck (d. 1787), Bohemian-German composer,*
> *when asked on his deathbed whether a tenor or bass*
> *should sing the role of Christ in* The Last Judgement

I will, whatever happens.

> *Johann Strauss (d. 1899), the king of Austrian*
> *waltzes, on being told to get some shut-eye*

You're the only one I like.

> *Percy Grainger (d. 1961), Australian composer.*
> *His last words were to Ella, his Swedish-born wife*

Now I have finished with all earthly business, and high time too. Yes, yes, my
dear child, now comes death.

> *Franz Lehar (d. 1948), Hungarian composer*

What the devil do you mean to sing to me, priest? You are out of tune.

> *Jean-Philippe Rameau (d. 1764), French composer, to his confessor*

The Final Curtain—
Show Business

Mama, if I get through this, I swear I'll be a better man.

> *Gene Vincent, the veteran rocker, famous for the 50s hit*
> *Bebop-A-Lula, after ten years of heavy drinking went*
> *home to his mother's trailer in a Los Angeles suburban trailer*
> *park to die of a bleeding ulcer. He didn't get through it*

I'd rather be skiing than doing this.

["Do you ski, Mr Laurel?"]

No, but I'd rather be doing that than doing this.

> *Stan Laurel (d. 1965), the thin one in the comedy duo Laurel*
> *and Hardy fame—born Arthur Stanley Jefferson, in England.*
> *The words were addressed to a nurse following a heart*
> *attack and shortly after he breathed his last*

I'm going to the can, Ginger.

> *Elvis Presley. Last words as reported by girlfriend Ginger Alden*

I'm shot; I'm shot.

> *John Lennon, after he was shot outside*
> *his New York apartment by deranged fan Mark Chapman;*
> *he staggered a few yards and uttered these words before falling.*

Yes, it's tough, but it's not as tough as doing comedy.

> *Edmund Gwenn (d. 1959), Hollywood actor, responding to the*
> *commiseration that it must be very hard for him, on his deathbed*

Codeine...bourbon.

> *Tallulah Bankhead (d. 1968)—dying words (allegedly) of the*
> *famous and proudly debauched movie actress*

This is it. I'm going, I'm going.

> *Al Jolson (d. 1950), American jazz singer*

Goodbye, kid. Hurry back.

> *Humphrey Bogart's actual last words to his wife Lauren Bacall, as*
> *he lay dying of cancer in their home in Los Angeles. She was*
> *about to leave to collect their children from Sunday School*

That was the best ice-cream soda I ever tasted.

> *Lou Costello (d. 1959), Hollywood actor. The funny half of the*
> *comedy team of Abbott and Costello had just enjoyed a*
> *strawberry ice-cream soda—two scoops*

We must stir ourselves. Move on! Work, work! Cover me! Must move on! Must
work! Cover me!

> *Eleanora Duse (d. 1924), Italian actress and* femme fatale.
> *She died in Pittsburgh, Pennsylvania*

Mamasha!

> *Vaslav Nijinsky (d. 1950), Russian ballet dancer. It translates as "Mama!"*

This isn't *Hamlet*, you know, it's not meant to go into the bloody ear.

> *Laurence Olivier (d. 1989), British actor,*
> *to a nurse who had spilt some water on him*

Oh, to die in Italy!

> *John Carradine (d. 1988), actor*

Don't pull down the blinds. I want the sunlight to greet me.

> *Rudolph Valentino (d. 1926). In this version of the silent-screen*
> *heartthrob's last words, Valentino stops a nurse who tries to*
> *close the drapes as he lies dying from peritonitis*

God damn the whole friggin' world and everyone in it but you, Carlotta.

> *W.C. Fields (d. 1946), American actor and comedian, to his*
> *mistress Carlotta Marti, before he died on Christmas Day 1946*

Why fear death? Death is only a beautiful adventure.

> *Charles Frohman (d. 1915), Broadway producer,*
> *quoting a line from* Peter Pan—*"To die will be an awfully big*
> *adventure"—as he went down with hundreds of other passengers*
> *on board the ship the* Lusitania *during World War I.*

Farewell, my friends! I am going to glory!

> *Isadora Duncan (d. 1927), dancer, as she stepped*
> *out of the Hotel Negresco in Nice and got in to the*
> *Bugatti sports car belonging to an admirer; the shawl she*
> *was wearing caught in the wheels, and broke her neck.*

I'll finally get to see Marilyn.

> *Joe DiMaggio, (attrib.) talking about his ex-wife*
> *Marilyn Monroe before his death in 1999*

Damn it...Don't you dare ask God to help me.

> *Joan Crawford (d. 1977), to her housekeeper*
> *who had begun to pray aloud*

No, I don't believe so.

> *Rock Hudson (d. 1985), Hollywood actor. (His last words were to*
> *Tom Clark, who had asked if he wanted a cup of coffee)*

Die? I should say not, my dear fellow. No Barrymore would ever allow such a
conventional thing to happen to him.

> *Commonly held to be the last words of John Barrymore (d. 1942),*
> *Hollywood actor, but they were words uttered by the tenacious*
> *actor to a friend during his final illness. His last words were, most*
> *probably, those addressed to his friend Gene Fowler: "Tell me,*
> *Gene, is it true that you're the illegitimate son of Buffalo Bill?"*

Are you happy? I'm happy.

> *Ethel (Blyth) Barrymore (d. 1959), the famous American*
> *actress, had been bedridden from rheumatism and a*
> *severe heart condition for some time. On June 17, 1959,*
> *she felt ill and asked for her doctor. After he left, she talked*
> *with her maid, Anna Albert, until she fell asleep. Barrymore*
> *awoke briefly the next morning and said to Anna: "Are*
> *you happy? I'm happy." She fell asleep again and died*
> *several hours later without regaining consciousness*

That was a great game of golf, fellas.

> *Bing Crosby (d. 1977), American singer,*
> *before collapsing on a Spanish golf course*

Nothing matters. Nothing matters.

> *Louis B. Mayer (d. 1957), Hollywood producer*

Do you know where I can get any s**t?

Lenny Bruce (d. 1966), comedian

I'm losin'.

Frank Sinatra (d. 1998). He spoke these last words to his wife, Barbara.

Doro, I can't breathe!

*Enrico Caruso (d. 1921), Italian tenor, as his once-famous lungs
failed him. (He died in Naples, his birthplace)*

How were the receipts tonight at Madison Square Garden?

Phineas Taylor Barnum (d. 1891), famous showman

I'm dying, I'm dying...he hurt me!

Virginia Rappe (d. 1921), Hollywood actress, referring to Fatty Arbuckle

I've had a hell of a lot of fun and I've enjoyed every minute of it.

*Errol Flynn (d. 1959), Hollywood actor in a
statement issued shortly before his death*

True glory is in virtue. Ah, I would willingly give all the applause I have received
to have performed one good action more.

Lupe de Vega (d. 1635), Spanish actor and dramatist

Curtain! Fast music! Light! Ready for the last finale! Great! The show looks good,
the show looks good!

> *Florenz Ziegfeld (d. 1932), American showman; on his deathbed*
> *he was imagining himself back at a "Follies" opening night*

Oh Mother, how beautiful it is!

> *Mary "Cholly Knickerbocker" Paul (d. 1942), New York gossip columnist*

Surprise me.

> *Bob Hope's (attrib.) reply to his son's question*
> *about where he wanted to be buried*

I love you Barbara...don't worry.

> *Cary Grant (d. 1986), Hollywood actor, to his wife as he was*
> *wheeled to intensive care following his stroke*

I love you, Betty...Betty.

> *Last words of Mario Lanza (d. 1959), opera singer—he had just*
> *finished talking to his wife Betty on the phone when he died*

Maria.

> *Last words of Nat "King" Cole (d. 1965), to a nurse in the hospital*
> *where he was dying of lung cancer. (Maria was his wife's name)*

Goodnight, my darlings. See you tomorrow.

> *Noel Coward (d. 1973), British dramatist, to his departing friends Graham*
> *Payn and Cole Lesley. He died of a heart attack later the same evening*

If this is what viral pneumonia does to one, I really don't think I shall bother to
have it again.

> *Gladys Cooper (d. 1971), British actress,*
> *peering into a mirror—she died the same night*

Put it down, hussy! Do you think I cannot help myself?

> *Mrs. David Garrick (d. 1822), dancer and wife of the famous English actor*
> *David Garrick. Aged 98, she retained a fiercely independent spirit; the above*
> *words were spoken while being offered a cup of tea by a servant*

My dear!

> *David Garrick (d. 1779), English actor,*
> *for whom the famous London theater is named*

Put your hands on my shoulders and don't struggle.

> *Sir William Gilbert (d. 1911), of Gilbert and Sullivan fame, who*
> *died while rescuing a girl drowning in the lake on his estate*

I can die now, I've lived twice.

> *Edith Piaf (d. 1963), the diminutive French*
> *singer known as "The Little Sparrow"*

Absolutely not!

> *Last words of Montgomery Clift (d. 1966), shouted through a*
> *bedroom door in response to carer Lorenzo James, who'd asked if he*
> *wanted to watch* The Misfits. *The actor was found dead on his bed the next*
> *morning—alcohol and drug dependency had precipitated his departure*

Wouldn't it be lovely if I could just go to sleep and not wake up again?

> *Kathleen Ferrier (d. 1953), British opera singer,*
> *to a nurse, as she lay dying of cancer*

Get my Swan costume ready.

> *Anna Pavlova (d. 1931), the Russian ballerina*
> *whose most famous role was as the Dying Swan*

Fancy being remembered around the world for the invention of a mouse!

> *Walt Disney (d. 1966), during his last illness*

Why should I talk to you? I've just been talking to your boss.

> *Wilson Mizner (d. 1933), jack of all trades (one of which was as a*
> *Hollywood impresario), to an attendant priest. To his physician,*
> *he quipped, "Well, doc, I guess this is the main event!"*

Why not? After all, it belongs to him.

> *Charlie Chaplin (d. 1977), when the attending priest muttered the*
> *words at his bedside, "May the Lord have mercy on your soul"*

Never felt better.

*Douglas Fairbanks, Sr. (d. 1939), was the premier swashbuckling
star of early Hollywood whose feature films included* Robin Hood,
The Thief of Bagdad, The Three Musketeers, *and* The Mark
of Zorro. *After returning from a football game, Fairbanks
became ill. A doctor prescribed total bed rest and Fairbanks
slept on and off through the next morning, awakening in the
afternoon to ask his attendant to open the window. "How
are you?" the attendant asked. Fairbanks answered with
a grin, rolled over, and went back to sleep. He died later that
night with his dog, Marco Polo, curled up at the foot of his bed*

" Meeting Their Makers—
Saints, Martyrs, and Those
Pure of Heart "

This side is roasted enough. Turn up, oh tyrant great, assay whether roasted or
raw thou thinkest the better meat.

> *Saint Lawrence (d. AD 285), an early Christian martyr*
> *who was put to death by being roasted on a griddle*

Let the flames come near me. I cannot burn!

> *Nicholas Ridley, protestant martyr who was*
> *burned at the stake by Mary Tudor in 1555*

Be of good comfort, Master Ridley, and play the man. We shall this day light
such a candle, by God's grace, in England, as I trust shall never be put out.

> *Hugh Latimer, protestant martyr, calling over to*
> *Nicolas Ridley on a neighboring pyre, in Oxford, England,*
> *where both men were burned as martyrs in 1555*

Hold the cross high so I may see it through the flames.

> *Joan of Arc, burned at the stake by English troops in France in 1431*

Let evil swiftly befall those who have wrongly condemned us. God will avenge us.

> *Jacques DeMolay (d. 1313), Master of the Order of the Knights Templar, who was imprisoned and executed on the orders of Pope Clement V and the French King Philip V ("the Fair"), who had accused the Templars of heresy. DeMolay was roasted to death*

Now comes the mystery.

> *Henry Ward Beecher (d. 1887), Congregationalist preacher. Earlier, when asked by his physician how high he could raise his arm, he said "Well, high enough to hit you, doctor"*

I have seen the glories of the world.

> *Isaac Barrow (d. 1677), English theologian and mathematician*

One!

> *Akiba Ben Joseph (d. AD 132), who was flayed alive by the Roman emperor Hadrian for having insisted upon the unity of the divine being*

I realise that patriotism is not enough. I must have no hatred or bitterness towards anyone.

> *Edith Cavell (d. 1915), the British nurse executed by a German firing squad for spying during World War I*

It is time for Matins.

> *Mystical poet St. John of the Cross (d. 1591), dying on*
> *the stroke of midnight, precisely as the bell began to toll*

Let me go. Let me go.

> *Clara Barton (d. 1912), "Angel of the Battlefield" and founder*
> *of the American Red Cross; she died at the age of 91. The*
> *epitaph on her gravestone is: "Nature has provided cure and*
> *final rest for all the heartache that mortals are called to endure"*

To be like Christ is to be a Christian.

> *William Penn (d. 1718), founder of Pennsylvania*

Always, always water for me.

> *Jane Addams (d. 1935), when offered alcohol to revive her. All her life she*
> *had been a social reformer and temperance campaigner*

I come. It is right. Wait a minute.

> *Alexander VI (d. 1503), pope and member of the*
> *powerful Borgia clan of medieval Florence, Italy*

Lord—open the King of England's eyes.

> *William Tyndale (d. 1536), protestant martyr and*
> *author of the first English translation of the Bible—*
> *he was burned at the stake, having been strangled first*

Pluck up thy spirits, man, and be not afraid to do thine office. My neck is
very short; take heed therefore and do not strike awry for the saving of
thine honesty.

> *Thomas More (d. 1535), English statesman, executed on the orders of*
> *Henry VIII. He had refused to bend to the will of the king in matters*
> *of religious conscience; later he was made a saint. These were his*
> *last words, directed to the executioner. On the way up to the scaffold,*
> *he had said, "I pray you, I pray you Mr Lieutenant, see me safely up.*
> *And for my coming down let me shift for myself"*

This hand having sinned in signing the writing must be the first to suffer
punishment. This hand hath offended.

> *Thomas Cranmer (d. 1556), architect of the Reformation under Henry VIII,*
> *but forced to recant under Mary I ("Bloody Mary"); later he went back*
> *on his statement, and as a result was burned at the stake for treason*
> *and heresy—yet he experienced the torments of guilt to the last*

I am prepared to die for Christ and His Church. I charge you in the name of the
Almighty not to hurt any other person here, for none of them has been
concerned in the late transactions.
In vain you menace me. If all the swords in England were brandishing over my
head, your terrors did not move me.

> *St Thomas a Becket, Archbishop of Canterbury and Christian martyr,*
> *assassinated in 1170 in Canterbury Cathedral, Kent, England, for having*
> *dared to challenge the authority of the English King Henry II*

A bishop ought to die on his legs.

John Woolton (d. 1594), who died as Bishop of Exeter

Amen.

Brigham Young (d. 1877), founder of the Mormon movement

I am reaching toward my inheritance.

Rev. Christopher P. Gadsen (d. 1805), American clergyman,
as he raised his arms heavenward

Build me a hut to die in. I am going home.

David Livingstone (d. 1873), Scottish explorer
and missionary, shortly before he died

Golgotha, Gethsemene.

John Heckewelder (d. 1823), missionary among the Ohio Indians

I see Earth receding. Heaven is opening. God is calling me.

Dwight Moody (d. 1899), American shoe salesman turned evangelist

My work is done. The pins of the tabernacle are taken out.

Charles Hodge (d. 1878), American theologian

There is no such thing as sudden death to a Christian.

Samuel Wilberforce (d. 1873), Bishop of Winchester

Heaven!

> *William Wilberforce (d. 1833), anti-slavery campaigner*

I have sinned against my brother, the ass.

> *St Francis of Assissi (d. 1226), founder of the Franciscan order. Medieval works of art often show the saint in communication with the animals*

God is my life.

> *Mary Baker Eddy (d. 1910), founder of the Christian Science movement*

God will help me. I am so tired.

> *Julia Ward Howe (d. 1910), US feminist and campaigner against slavery. She was also the author of* Hymn of the Republic (Mine eyes have seen the glory of the coming of the Lord), *which she composed at the start of the American Civil War and which is sung to the tune of "John Brown's Body"*

Will not all my riches save me? What! Is there no bribing death?

> *Cardinal Henry Beaufort (d. 1447)*

It is a great mystery, but I shall know all soon.

> *George Peabody (d. 1869), English philanthropist*

John Rodgers did.

> *Last words of John Holmes, who had awoken momentarily from his coma to hear his nurse saying, "No one ever died with warm feet." To which came the above reply—and Holmes never spoke another word. John Rodgers was an early Protestant martyr who was burned at the stake*

Don't worry, be happy.

> *Meher Baba (d. 1969)—the words were spoken in 1925, after which time his lips remained sealed for good, which turned out to be the next 44 years...*

I am going where all tears will be wiped away.

> *Matthew Cotton (d. 1728), one of the early American fathers and a descendant of John Cotton, the famous English puritan who fled to America to escape the wrath of an archbishop for refusing to kneel at the sacrament*

I have loved justice and hated iniquity; therefore I die in exile.

> *Pope Gregory VII (d. 1085) was in direct conflict with the Holy Roman Emperor, Henry IV, eventually excommunicating him. In response, Henry launched his forces against the pope and besieged Rome from 1081–1083, finally conquering the city in 1084. Gregory fled to the castle of St. Angelo for safety. Gregory's ally Robert Guiscard rescued the pope from St. Angelo, but much of Rome was destroyed in the process. Gregory was force to flee Rome and take refuge in Salerno, where he died the following year*

O, holy simplicity!

> *John Huss (d. 1415) was a Czech priest who became the leader of a reform religious movement. He antagonized the archbishop and clergy of Prague and was forbidden to preach and finally excommunicated. He was tricked by the Holy Roman Emperor, Sigismund, into attending a reform council. There, he was arrested, condemned as a heretic, and burned at the stake*

The Road to Perdition—
Sinners

Haircut!

> *Albert Anastasia (d. 1957), gangster, shot while in a barber's chair*

There were seven Democrats in Hinsdale County! But you, yah voracious, main-eatin' son of a bitch, ate five of them, therefore I sentence you t' be hanged by the neck until you're dead, dead, dead!

> *Sentencing Judge to one Alfred Packer, who shot and ate his gold-prospecting companions in 1873. The death sentence was commuted to a prison term. Packer's dying words, according to the Littleton* Independent *were "I'm not guilty of the charge"*

I've been looking forward to this.

> *Edgar Edwards, on his way to the scaffold where he was hanged for having committed a double murder in 1902; at his trial there had been (unheeded) pleas of insanity*

What a thrill it will be to die in the electric chair... the supreme thrill, the only one I haven't tried.

> *Albert Fish, sadistic child killer and cannibal, before his*
> *execution in said electric chair in 1936. Fish needed a*
> *number of operations to remove corroded needles from*
> *his private parts before he was sent to the chair, yet still*
> *managed to short circuit it first time round*

I am going to the Lordy...

> *Charles Jules Guiteau (d. 1882), assassin of President Garfield,*
> *as he was hanged for the crime. He was reciting a line from a*
> *poem he had composed the morning of his death*

Hurrah for anarchy! This is the happiest moment of my life.

> *George Engel (d. 1887), before being executed for*
> *his part in the Haymarket Riots of May 4, 1886*
> *in Chicago. All four anarchists were hanged;*
> *the fifth, Louis Lingg, committed suicide by*
> *lighting a stick of dynamite in his mouth*

I love you.

> *Sean Flannagan (d. 1989), to his executioner,*
> *before being killed by lethal injection in New York*

Long live Germany...Argentina...I greet my wife, my family and my friends. I had
  to obey the rules of war and my flag.

> *Adolf Eichmann (d. 1962), before he was hanged for war crimes.*
> *The Nazi officer had escaped to Argentina after the war, but was*
> *tracked down and arrested in 1960*

I'd rather be fishing.

> *Jimmy Glass (d. 1987), before being executed*
> *by lethal injection in Louisiana*

You can be a king or a street sweeper, but everyone dances with the Grim
  Reaper.

> *Robert Alton Harris (d. 1992), executed in California's gas chamber*

I am innocent, innocent, innocent. Make no mistake about this. I owe society
  nothing. I am an innocent man and something very wrong is taking place
  tonight.

> *Lionel Herrera (d. 1993), before being executed by lethal injection in Texas*

I don't hold any grudges. This is my doing. Sorry it happened.

> *Steven Judy (d. 1981), executed in the electric chair, Indiana*

Such is life.

> *Ned Kelly (d. 1880), famous Australian bushranger executed by hanging*

Today is a good day to die. I forgive all of you. I hope God does too.

Mario Benjamin Murphy (d. 1997),
before being executed by lethal injection in Texas

Capital punishment: them without the capital get the punishment.

John Spenkelink (d. 1979), executed in the electric chair, Florida

I killed the President because he was the enemy of the good people, the good
working people. I am not sorry for my crime.

Leon Czolgosz (d. 1902), who assassinated President McKinley during a
Pan-American Exposition in 1901, and was hanged for his crime

It is no shame to stand on this scaffold. I served my fatherland as others
before me.

Karl Brandt (d. 1946), Nazi general, about to be hanged
for war crimes following the Nuremburg trials

A thousand years will pass and the guilt of Germany will not be erased.

Hans Frank (d. 1946), Nazi war criminal who was hanged for his crimes
following the Nuremberg trials. Frank had converted to Catholicism
following his arrest. When asked for his final statement before his
execution, he whispered, "I ask God to accept me with mercy"

God save Germany! My last wish is that Germany rediscover her unity and that
an alliance is made between East and West and that peace reign on earth.

Joachim Von Ribbentrop (d. 1946), Nazi war criminal, hanged for his crimes

Dear Germany.

*Hermann Hoefle (d. 1962), Nazi general who had gone
unpunished after the war. However, his past caught up with him
and he committed suicide in a Viennese prison before he could be tried*

Vive La France!

*Pierre Laval (d. 1945), prime minister of France and collaborator
with the Nazi occupiers during World War II—he was shot*

You sons of bitches. Give my love to Mother.

*Francis "Two Gun" Crowley (d. 1931), robber
and murderer, before dying in the electric chair*

It don't matter—I figure I licked the Rock anyway.

*Bernard Coy (d. 1946), murderer, seconds before being
shot by guards while attempting to escape from Alcatraz*

I'm going down with my six-guns.

Joel Collins (d. 1877), outlaw and member of the Sam Bass gang

Don't draw it too tight. I can't breathe...Long live anarchy...This is the happiest
moment of my life.

> *Adolf Fischer (d. 1887), one of the five "Chicago Anarchists," before his*
> *execution by hanging for his part in the Haymarket Riots in Chicago in 1886*

Who the hell tipped you off? I'm Floyd, all right. You got me this time.

> *Charles "Pretty Boy" Floyd (d. 1934), cornered by*
> *FBI agents after committing another bank robbery*

I will throw up my hands for no gringo dog.

> *"Three Fingered Jack" Garcia, bandit, allegedly killed in 1853*

Let's do it.

> *Gary Gilmore (d. 1977)—last words of the first man*
> *to be executed in Utah after the US Supreme Court*
> *had lifted its 1970 suspension of the death penalty*

I'll be in hell before you're finished breakfast, boys...let her rip!

> *"Black Jack" Ketchum (d. 1901), bank robber*
> *and murderer, executed by hanging*

Yes, and I'm going to end it here.

> *Outlaw Harvey Logan, a.k.a. "Kid Curry" (d. 1903), asked by a fellow*
> *outlaw whether he'd been hit. Logan then turned his gun on himself*

Some day they will go down together
And they will bury them side by side
To a few it means grief
To the law it's relief
But it's death to Bonnie and Clyde.

> *Bonnie Parker (d. 1934), one half of the infamous*
> *bank-robbing duo—this was the last verse of the final*
> *poem she wrote, which she titled "The Story of Suicide Sal"*

What is the scaffold? A shortcut to heaven.

> *Charles Peace (d. 1879), murderer, executed by hanging*

Me mudder did it!

> *Arnold Rothstein (d. 1928), gangster and financial whizz-kid,*
> *a.k.a. "Mr Big," when asked by police who had gunned him*
> *down —in other words, refusing to the last to name his killer*

I will be glad to discuss this proposition with my attorney, and that after I talk
with one, we could either discuss it with him or discuss it with my attorney if
the attorney thinks it is a wise thing to do, but at the present time I have
nothing more to say to you.

> *Lee Harvey Oswald to Inspector Thomas Kelly*

Men, the next time you lift a glass of whiskey, I want you to look into the bottom
   of the glass and see if there isn't a hangman's noose in it, like the
   one here.

> Boudinot "Bood" Crumpton (d. 1891), sentenced to hang at Fort Smith,
> Arkansas, for having shot dead his traveling companion while under the
> influence of liquor. (He issued these words of warning from the scaffold)

Jack...

> Neil Cream (d. 1929), sentenced to hang—at the last moment,
> it's thought he began to confess to the Ripper murders

In this farewell letter to the world, written as I face eternity, I say that Ethel le
   Neve loved me as few women love men and that her innocence of any crime,
   save that of yielding to the dictates of her heart, is absolute. My last prayer
   will be that God will protect her and keep her safe from harm and allow her to
   join me in eternity.

> "Dr." Hawley Harvey Crippen (d. 1910), in his last letter before being hanged
> for the murder of his wife Cora. Ethel le Neve was acquitted

Ah, you might make that a double.

> Neville Heath (d. 1946), murderer, asking for a last
> whiskey before being executed by hanging

As God is my witness, I was responsible for the deaths of only two women.

I didn't kill Minnie Williams. Minnie killed her!

> *Herman Webster Mudgett (d. 1896), America's most prolific murderer;*
> *he was charged with the deaths of at least 200 women and hanged*
> *for his crimes—though he protested his innocence to the last*

We are the first victims of American fascism.

> *Ethel Rosenberg (d. 1953), gassed for (alleged) spying offences*

I am going to be face to face with Jesus now. I love you all very much. I will see you all when you get there. I will wait for you.

> *Karla Faye Tucker Brown, (d. 1998) executed by lethal injection for the*
> *murder of two people in 1983. She had become a devout born-again*
> *Christian during her time on death row, prompting calls for clemency*

This is funny.

> *Doc Holliday, as he lay dying in 1887. The legendary*
> *gunfighter was regarding his own bare feet, amazed that*
> *he was dying in bed of tuberculosis and not with his boots on*

Who's out there?

> *William Bonney, a.k.a. "Billy the Kid" (d. 1881)—Sheriff Pat Garrett*
> *was out there, and he shot Billy dead moments later*

Helen, please take me out. I will settle the incident. Come on, open the soak
duckets; the chimney sweeps. Talk to the sword. Shut up, you got a big
mouth! Please help me to get up. Henry! Max! Come over here. French
Canadian bean soup. I want to pay. Let them leave me alone.

> *The (recorded) last ravings of Chicago gangster*
> *"Dutch Schultz," shot and fatally wounded in 1935*

I am the master of my fate;
I am the captain of my soul.

> *The last words of Timothy McVeigh, perpetrator of the Oklahoma*
> *bombing in June 2001. He was quoting from the poem* Invictus,
> *written by the nineteenth-century English poet William Ernest Henley*

Shoot straight you bastards and don't make a mess of it!

> *Last words of Harry Harbord "Breaker" Morant (d. 1902),*
> *Australian national hero, executed by firing squad*

I am reconciled to my death but I detest the mode.

> *John André (d. 1780), British spy executed during the American Revolution.*
> *He had just caught sight of the hangman's noose, having thought he would*
> *be executed by firing squad. He then added, "It will be but a momentary*
> *pang. I pray you bear witness that I have met my fate like a brave man"*

Death itself isn't dreadful, but hanging seems an awkward way of entering the
adventure.

> *Gerald Chapman (d. 1926), executed for killing a policeman*

Take lots of pictures! We are the revolutionaries!

>*James McLain (d. 1970), American criminal, moments before*
>*being shot as he made an attempted escape during his trial*

All right! Go ahead!

>*Arizona "Ma" Baker (d. 1935), bank robber—she was giving the*
>*order for her sons to start the fatal shootout with the F. B. I.*

Nothing succeeds with me. Even here I meet with disappointment.

>*Ryumin Michael Bestuzhev (d. 1826), Russian revolutionary,*
>*after the rope set up to hang him had broken*

No, but don't keep me waiting any longer than necessary.

>*John Brown (d. 1859), abolitionist, asked on the scaffold if he was tired*

I have a right to be curious; I have never seen one before. It is the toilette of
death, but it leads to immortality.

>*Charlotte Corday (d. 1793), staring at the guillotine by*
>*which she was condemned to die for the assassination*
>*of the French revolutionary leader Marat*

If I am to be killed, let Adolf do it himself.

>*Ernst Roehm (d. 1934), head of the Nazi SA (Sturm Abteilung), assassinated*
>*on Hitler's orders as part the Führer's "Night of the Long Knives"*

I want that 50 bucks you owe me—and I want it now!

> *Carl "Alfalfa" Switzer (d. 1959), one time star of the film series* Our Gang; *he later went to seed and was shot in a bar brawl following the above rash demand of repayment from a creditor, who happened to be armed*

If anybody passes, they'll see me.

> *Jesse James (d. 1882), train robber*

Goodbye boys! I die a true American!

> *"Bill the Butcher" Poole (d. 1855), American gang leader and head of New York's Bowery Boys—he became a changed man on his deathbed*

I guess you were right, Wyatt. I can't see a damn thing.

> *Morgan Earp, as he died at the gunfight at the OK Corral in 1882. His final words were in agreement with his atheistic brother who had declared there was no life after death*

It is all the same in the end.

> *Titus Oates (d. 1705), instigator of the "Popish Plot"*

He doesn't know who I am.

> *Heinrich Himmler (d. 1945), Head of the Gestapo, referring to the interrogating sergeant after his arrest by British forces. The latter were unable to prevent the Nazi officer from breaking a capsule of cyanide—one of the so-called "SS Cough Drops"—in his mouth and swallowing it*

Had I but served my God with half the zeal I served my King, He would not in
mine age have left me naked to mine enemies.

> *The last words of Thomas Cardinal Wolsey (d. 1530), according*
> *to the play* Henry VIII, *Act III, scene (ii), by William Shakespeare.*
> *Shakespeare would have found them in the* Chronicles *(1577) by*
> *Raphael Holinshed: "If I had served God as diligently as I have*
> *done the King, He would not have given me over in my gray hairs."*

Well, gentlemen. You are about to see a baked Appel.

> *George Appel, moments before being*
> *executed in the electric chair in New York, 1928*

How about this for a headline for tomorrow's paper? French fries.

> *James French, executed by electric chair in Oklahoma, 1966*

Why yes. A bullet-proof vest.

> *Final request of James Rodgers (d. 1960), notorious murderer,*
> *before his execution by a firing squad*

Tell mother I died for my country. I have done what I thought was for the best.
Useless! Useless!

> *John Wilkes Booth (d. 1865), the assassin of Abraham Lincoln,*
> *as he was about to breathe his last thanks to a bullet*
> *received during the hunt by soldiers to arrest him*

The world is bobbing around.

> *Sam Bass (d. 1878), American desperado mortally wounded by the Texas*
> *Rangers in Round Rock, Texas, as he arrived to rob a bank*

I wish the whole human race had one neck and I had my hands on it.

> *Extract from a letter sent by Carl Panzram, mass murderer,*
> *to the Society for the Abolition of Capital Punishment,*
> *whose efforts to save his life went unappreciated—unrepentant*
> *to the last, he said he was positively looking forward to the day of*
> *his execution. He was hanged in Leavenworth, Kansas, in 1930.*
> *Panzram's actual last words were, "Hurry it up, you Hoosier*
> *bastard! I could hang a dozen men while you're screwing around"*

I did not get my Spaghetti-O's; I got spaghetti. I want the press to know this.

> *Last words of Thomas J. Grasso, before his execution*
> *by lethal injection in Oklahoma in 1995*

I'd like to thank my family for loving me and taking care of me...And the rest of
the world can kiss my ass.

> *Johnny Frank Garrett, before his execution*
> *by lethal injection in Texas in 1992*

Gentlemen, don't hang me high for the sake of decency. I am afraid I shall fall.

> *Mary Blandy (d. 1752), on the scaffold. She was*
> *hanged for having murdered her own father*

The King is Dead—
Royalty and Aristocrats

Stay for the sign.

> Charles I, King of England, to his executioner on the scaffold at
> which he was beheaded in 1649. The "sign" was the moment the
> king stretched out his arms before him, his neck on the execution
> block, to signal that he was ready—the blow followed swiftly

Is it my birthday or am I dying?

> Nancy, Lady Astor (d. 1964), surprised at seeing
> all her family gathered around her bed

Mine eyes desire thee only. Farewell.

> Catherine of Aragon (d. 1536), ill-fated first wife of King Henry VIII, in her
> final letter to her former husband as she lay dying of cancer. Her actual
> dying words were, "Lord into Thy hands I commend my spirit"

Yes, I have heard of it. I am very glad.

> *Edward VII (d. 1910), King of England, on being told by his son that*
> *one of his horses had won at Kempton Park, the famous English*
> *racetrack; shortly after, the king fell into a coma from which he*
> *never awoke. As he lost consciousness, he is said to have murmured,*
> *"No, I shall not give in. I shall go on. I shall work to the end"*

I see that you have made three spelling mistakes.

> *Thomas de Mahay, Marquis de Favras (d. 1790),*
> *as he was handed his official death sentence on his way*
> *to the guillotine during the French Revolution*

Liebes Frauchen.

> *Albert, Prince Consort (d. 1861), to Queen Victoria his wife,*
> *as he lay dying of typhoid fever. Earlier, he had asked her,*
> *"You have not forgotten the important communication to Nemours?*
> *Good little woman." Albert's farewell to the nation was fittingly public-*
> *spirited: "I have had wealth, rank and power, but if these were all, how*
> *wretched I should be. 'Rock of ages cleft for me; Let me hide myself in thee'"*

Shame, shame on a conquered king!

> *Henry II (d. 1189), King of England, enraged, even on his*
> *deathbed, that his sons had headed the conspirators who were*
> *plotting against him, joining the King of France to defeat him in battle.*
> *Yet this was also the king who had ordered the murder of Thomas A. Becket*

You are going to hurt me. Please don't hurt me. Just one more moment,
executioner, a small moment, I beg you!

> *Madame du Barry (d. 1793), mistress of the defunct*
> *French King Louis XV, pleading with her executioner as she*
> *approached the guillotine during the French Revolution*

I desire to leave to the men that come after me a remembrance of me in
good works.

> *Alfred the Great (d. 899), the Saxon King of Wessex, England*

What a beautiful day—

> *Alexander I (d. 1825), Tsar of Russia. His death was hastened by a broken*
> *heart, caused by the death of his illegitimate daughter a year earlier*

What have I done, or my children, that I should meet such a fate? And from your
hands, too, you who have met with friendship and kindness from my people,
who have received nothing but benefits from my hands?

> *Atahualpa (d. 1533), last of the Incas, on being condemned to*
> *burn at the stake by Pizarro, the infamous Spanish* conquistador

Walty, what is this? It is death, my boy. You have deceived me.

> *George IV (d. 1830), King of England, to his page, Sir Walthen Waller*

The executioner is, I believe, very expert...And my neck is very slender. Oh God, have pity on my soul! Oh God, have pity on my soul! Oh God, have pity...

> *Anne Boleyn (d. 1536), the second wife of English King*
> *Henry VIII, who was executed in the "French manner"*
> *that is by a skilled swordsman not by an axe-man*

I pray you, gentlemen, in the name of modesty, suffer me to cover my bosom.

> *Madame Elizabeth, sister of the executed*
> *King Louis XVI— she was guillotined in 1797*

Sophie, Sophie, don't die—live for our children.

> *Franz Ferdinand, Archduke of Austria, assassinated*
> *by a Serbian revolutionary at Sarajevo in 1914—an event*
> *that sparked World War I. On receiving his mortal wound,*
> *he had famously declared, "It is nothing, it is nothing"*

I am tired of ruling over slaves. We are over the mountain; we shall go better now.

> *Frederick the Great (d. 1786), King of Prussia*

No, not quite naked—I shall have my uniform on.

> *Frederick William I (d. 1740), King of Prussia and father of*
> *Frederick the Great, on hearing the priest's words "Naked came I*
> *out of my mother's womb, and naked shall I return..." Surveying*
> *his own coffin, he said, "I shall sleep right well there"*

It is nothing.

> *Henry IV (d. 1610), King of France, assassinated by a*
> *mad monk by the name of Ravaillac*

All is lost. Monks! Monks! Monks! So, now all is gone—empire, body, soul.

> *Henry VIII (d. 1547), King of England, who died having worked*
> *his way through five different wives—and the sixth, survived him*

Pray, hasten thy office...I die a queen, but I would rather die the wife of
  Culpepper. God have mercy on my soul. Good people, I beg you, pray for me.

> *Catherine Howard (d. 1542), fifth wife of Henry VIII; she was executed for*
> *having conducted adulterous affairs, which was a treasonable offence*

Youth, I forgive thee. Take off his chains, give him one hundred shillings and
  let him go.

> *Richard I (d. 1199), "The Lionheart," King of England, killed by an*
> *archer (one Bertrand de Gourdon) during a siege in France. He*
> *had the man brought before him and forgave him. Then he died.*
> *Nonetheless, his second-in-command had the archer executed*

The devil do with it! It will end as it began; it came with a lass and it will go
  with a lass.

> *James V (d. 1542), King of Scotland*

Fie on the horror!

> *Princesse de Lamballe (d. 1792), close companion of Marie*
> *Antoinette, killed by the mob during the French Revolution; this*
> *was her response when told to yell "Vive la Nation!"*

I am a queen, but I have not power to move my arms.

> *Louise, Queen of Prussia (d. 1810)*

When I am dead and opened, you shall find "Calais" lying in my heart.

> *Mary Tudor (d. 1558), Queen of England, whose*
> *religious persecutions earned her the epithet "Bloody Mary."*
> *Calais, once an English enclave, had been lost to the French*

Do not cry, I have prayed for you. In You, Lord, I have faith, and You shall protect
me for ever. Into Thy hands, O Lord, I commend my spirit.

> *Mary, Queen of Scots, executed in 1587 on the*
> *orders of Elizabeth I, Queen of England*

I will die King of England. I will not budge a foot! Treason! Treason!

> *Richard III (d. 1485), King of England, killed at the Battle of*
> *Bosworth Field. He was rushing to attack Henry Tudor, at the*
> *head of the Lancastrian forces, when he was cut down*

I am very tired.

> *Lola Montez (d. 1861), onetime mistress of King Ludwig I of Bavaria*
> *(who also made her a countess). And it was no wonder, after a lifetime*
> *of dancing, adventuring, and royal concubinage. (The Broadway line*
> *"What Lola wants, Lola gets" originated with the fiery Lola Montez)*

Be careful not to let eunuchs meddle in government affairs. The Ming dynasty
was brought to ruin by eunuchs, and its fate should be a warning to
my people.

> *Tzu-Hsi (d. 1908), Empress of China*

Oh, that peace may come. Bertie!

> *Queen Victoria (d. 1901), referring to the son who had caused her so much*
> *heartache and whom she had just embraced on her deathbed*

There are six guineas for you. And do not hack me as you did my Lord Russell.

> *Duke of Monmouth (d. 1685), to his executioner.*
> *James Scott, Duke of Monmouth, was the illegitimate son of*
> *Charles II; he had led an unsuccessful rebellion again James II,*
> *culminating in the Battle of Sedgemoor, where he was defeated*

My God, my God! I am sadly wounded! Have mercy on me, and on my poor
people!

> *William of Orange (d. 1584), founder of the Dutch republic—and*
> *nicknamed "The Silent"—as he was shot by an assassin*

[Are] your great buttocks grown any less or no?

> *The sixteenth-century Lord Thomas Seymour, writing*
> *to the former object of his sexual ardor—it was a crass and*
> *foolish indiscretion, as the object of his attentions had grown*
> *into Queen Elizabeth I of England, the "Virgin Queen." Of*
> *Thomas Seymour (husband of Katherine Parr, her de-facto*
> *stepmother) Elizabeth made the famous remark that he was a*
> *man "of great wit but little judgement." She had him beheaded*

I have deserved a thousand deaths.

> *John Dudley (d. 1553), Duke of Northumberland, executed for his part in the*
> *conspiracy to place Lady Jane Grey on the throne of England*

I will not be a duke, I will be king.

> *Thus sobbed a petulant Lord Guildford Dudley, consort to Lady*
> *Jane Grey, after she had informed him that she would not be*
> *making him king. She had been duped by his ambitious father,*
> *the Duke of Northumberland, into marrying him. Both Dudley and*
> *Lady Jane, the "Queen of Nine Days," were executed by Queen*
> *Mary I on the latter's accession to the throne of England*

At least I shall have one comfort in having my eyes eternally closed—I shall
never see that monster again.

> *The dying Queen Caroline of Ansbach, wife and consort*
> *of the English King George II, as she lay dying in 1737.*
> *She was referring to her eldest son Frederick Louis*

Try if you cannot tinker me up to last over that date.

> *The English King William IV (d. 1837), begging his doctor to*
> *do all in his power to help him live to see another anniversary of the*
> *Battle of Waterloo (June 18). The king died two days after the anniversary*

How is the empire?

> *The official version of the dying King George V's final utterance,*
> *printed in* The Times *newspaper the day after his death,*
> *which happened on January 20, 1936. Also quoted as his final words*
> *is the sentence, to his Privy Councilors, "Gentlemen, I am sorry for*
> *keeping you waiting like this—I am unable to concentrate," (he was*
> *having difficulty signing his initials). However, "Bugger Bognor!" is the*
> *third, altogether more plausible version; the king was responding to his*
> *physician, who claimed that His Highness would soon be back in the*
> *seaside resort where he had spent earlier spells of convalescence*

I have now got an asthma. Open the window, pray.

> *The dying words of Queen Caroline (d. 1821) of Brunswick,*
> *wife and consort of the English King George IV*

And let not poor Nelly starve.

> *Charles II (d. 1685) on his deathbed, concerned about the future welfare*
> *of his mistress, the actress Nell Gwyn. Ever courteous, the king also*
> *said, apologetically to his advisors gathered at his bedside, "I have*
> *been a most unconscionable time a-dying, but I hope you will excuse it"*

Has God forgotten everything I've done for him?

> *Louis XIV (d. 1715), the "Sun King." His actual last words—uttered*
> *on August 31, 1715, before sliding into unconsciousness—are reported*
> *to have been, "Now and at the hour of my death, help me, oh God." He*
> *died in his sleep on September 1, 1715. Earlier, Louis also said to*
> *an attendant weeping at his bedside: "Why do you weep? Did you*
> *think I should live for ever? I thought dying had been harder"*

Good! A woman who can fart is not dead!

> *The Comtesse de Vercelles, with whom the*
> *French Enlightenment author Jean-Jacques Rousseau*
> *spent part of his early youth. In his autobiographical*
> Confessions, *Rousseau wrote, "In the agonies of death she broke*
> *wind loudly. 'Good!' she said, 'A woman who can fart is not dead!'"*

Spain, My God!

> *Alfonso XIII (d. 1941), King of Spain, who went into exile*
> *in 1931, never to return to his native soil; two weeks before*
> *his death he had abdicated in favor of his third son*

If I feel in good form, I shall take the difficult way up; if I do not, I shall take the easy one. I shall join you in an hour.

> *Albert I (d. 1934), King of Belgium, to his companions on the Rocher de*
> *Marches les Dames, a massif in Belgium on which he fell to his death*

Use it for the good of my people.

>*Anne, Queen of England (d. 1714), handing the*
>*symbolic staff of the treasury to Lord Shrewsbury*

All my possessions for one moment of time.

>*Acknowledged as having been the last words of Queen Elizabeth I (d. 1603).*
>*Earlier, to Robert Cecil, who told the Queen she must rest, she is recorded as*
>*having declared: "Must! Is must a word to be addressed to princes? Little*
>*man, little man! Thy father, if he had been alive, durst not have used that*
>*word. Thou art so presumptuous, for thou knowest I shall die"*

May my blood cement the happiness of Fr—

>*Louis XVI of France's final, shouted words, before his*
>*death at the guillotine in 1793. From the scaffold, moments earlier,*
>*he had declared, "I die innocent of all the crimes of which I am charged.*
>*I forgive those who are guilty of my death, and I pray God that the*
>*blood which you are about to shed may never be required of France."*
>*The rest of his speech was drowned out in the roll of drums*

I submit.

>*William III (d. 1702), Prince of Orange, later King of England,*
>*to his attending physicians. Moments before he had said to*
>*them, "I know that you have done all that skill and learning*
>*could do for me; but the case is beyond your art"*

What dost thou fear? Strike, man, strike!

Sir Walter Raleigh (d. 1618), English courtier, voyager, and adventurer, who rose to fame during the reign of Elizabeth I, addressing his executioner who was about to behead him. Raleigh had fallen out of favor on the accession of Elizabeth's successor, James I, to the throne of England. Moments before, the executioner had asked which way he wanted his head to face, east or west, to which Raleigh had replied, "So the heart be right; it is no matter which way the head lieth." Earlier, Raleigh had asked the executioner to show him the ax, along whose blade he ran his finger, with the now-famous comment, "Tis a sharp remedy, but a sure one for all ills." Earlier still, he had said to a friend trying to approach the scaffold, "I know not how it may be with you, but I shall be sure to find a place." Gallows humor to the last

Give Dayrolles a chair.

> *Earl of Chesterfield (d. 1773), close confidante of English men of letters Jonathan Swift and Alexander Pope—and ever-courteous and polite, right to the end. This last visitor was Dayrolles, his godson*

A king should die standing.

> *Louis XVIII (d. 1824), king of France (brother of the guillotined French king Louis XVI), echoing the words of the Roman emperor Vespasian as he struggled to rise from his bed*

That manner of death has my full approval.

> *Prince Felix Schwartzenberg of Austria (d. 1852) to his*
> *doctor who had warned him that he would have a stroke if he*
> *carried on in the same way, which he did regardless*

James, present my compliments to Lord Erne and tell him it will be a dead heat
between us.

> *Lord Norbury (d. 1831), English aristocrat, asking on*
> *his deathbed for a message to be taken to another elderly*
> *aristocrat whose end was also fast approaching*

Well I fooled 'em for five years!

> *Lord Duveen (d. 1939), English art collector. He died at Claridges*
> *Hotel in London. The words were addressed to his nurse, and*
> *referred to the fact that his illness had been a long one*

One moment, Monsieur le Curé, and we will leave together.

> *Madame de Pompadour (d. 1764), mistress and then companion*
> *of the French King Louis XV. She was speaking to her confessor,*
> *who had risen to take his leave, upon which movement she died*

I have caused more than a hundred thousand masses to be said for the repose of
unhappy souls, so that I flatter myself I have not been a very bad Christian.

> *King Louis XV (d. 1774), who had been a particularly pleasure-*
> *driven and depraved French king and not a very good Christian*

No. Open a bottle for yourself and the nurse.

Lady Emerald Cunard (d. 1948), English socialite, on being offered a small sip of champagne as she lay dying

Dear papa...

Princess Alice (d. 1878) from diptheria—Princess Alice was daughter to Queen Victoria and her main emotional support when Prince Albert died. Her own children suffered many tragedies; Elizabeth married Sergei the Grand Duke of Russia and was murdered by Russian bolsheviks in 1918, Alexandra married Tsar Nicholas and was execcuted in 1918, while daughter Victoria's son, Louis Mountbatten, was murdered by Irish terrorists in 1979

Fading into the Sunset—
Great Artists

I have offended God and mankind because my work did not reach the quality it
   should have.

> *Last words of Leonardo da Vinci (d.1519), artist,*
> *inventor, and all-round "Renaissance man"*

It's very beautiful, but I want to go farther away.

> *Augustus Saint-Gaudens (d. 1907),*
> *Irish-born American sculptor, while watching a sunset*

You are wrong not to marry. It's useful.

> *Pablo Picasso (d. 1973), Spanish-born giant of twentieth-century*
> *art. He was addressing these words to his doctor, a bachelor,*
> *while holding out his hand to his second wife, Jacqueline.*
> *His last words have also been recorded as "Drink to me"*

[I have enjoyed] a world which, though wicked enough in all conscience, is
perhaps as good as worlds unknown.

John James Audubon (d. 1851), American naturalist painter

I should desire that the last words which I should pronounce in this Academy,
and from this place, might be the name of Michelangelo.

*Sir Joshua Reynolds's farewell words to the Royal Academy, over which
he presided as its first president. He died in 1792. The last thing he
was heard to say was, "I know that all things must have an end"*

We are all going to heaven and Van Dyke is of the party.

*Thomas Gainsborough (d. 1788), British painter, to Joshua
Reynolds, who was visiting him on his deathbed. The phrase was
recorded by Gainsborough's friend William Jackson*

To judge by what I am now endure, the hand of death grasps me strongly.

Salvator Rosa (d.1673), Italian painter famous for his wild landscapes

I am curious to see what happens in the next world to one who dies unshriven.

*Pietro Perugino (d.1523), Italian Renaissance painter, giving his
reason for refusing to see a priest as he lay dying*

Happy.

*Raphael, properly called Raffaello Sanzio (d. 1520),
Italian painter of the High Renaissance period*

The sun, my dear, the sun is God.

> *J. M. W. Turner (d.1851), English painter*
> *famous for his landscapes and much admired*
> *by the Impressionists for his use of light*

Pontier. Pontier.

> *Paul Cézanne (d.1906), who died in the town of Aix-en-Provence*
> *in the south of France—where Monsieur Pontier was curator of*
> *the museum that had failed to display the painter's work*

I hope with all my heart there will be painting in heaven.

> *Jean-Baptiste Camille Corot (d.1875), French painter*

Monsieur le Curé, I'm happier to see you now than I shall be in a few days when
   you come with your little bell.

> *Henri de Toulouse Lautrec (d.1901), French artist; he died of syphilis at the*
> *age of 36. He died on the same day as the visit by the local priest, "le Curé"*

Wonderful, wonderful, this death!

> *William Etty (d.1849), English painter*

If I had strength to hold a pen, I would write down how easy and pleasant a
   thing it is to die.

> *Dr. William Hunter (d. 1783), Scottish anatomist and art collector*

I live alone and miserable, trapped as marrow under the bark of the tree. My voice is like a wasp caught in a bag of skin and bones. My teeth shake and rattle like the keys of a musical instrument. My face is a scarecrow. My ears never cease to buzz. In one of them, a spider weaves its web, in the other one, a cricket sings all night long. My rattling catarrh won't let me sleep. This is the state where art has led me, after granting me glory. Poor, old, beaten, I will be reduced to nothing, if death does not come swiftly to my rescue. Pains have quartered me, torn me, broken me and death is the only inn awaiting me.

Michelangelo (d.1564), not a deathbed utterance, but the thoughts of a dying man who continued to labor alone, at night, because the pain of sleeping was too much to bear

Last Known Address— Leaders

Et tu, Brute?—Then fall Caesar.

> Gaius Julius Caesar. The Roman Emperor was surprised that his friend
> Brutus should be among the assassins. Caesar died in 44 BC

I am still alive!

> Gaius Caligula, as reported by the Roman historian Tacitus. The
> notoriously crazy Roman Emperor made the injudicious last
> remark while being stabbed to death by his own guards in AD 41

Smite my womb! Level your rage against the womb which gave birth to such a
monster!

> Agrippina (d. AD 59), unfortunate mother of Nero, Roman
> emperor, who ordered her to be stabbed to death

Little urn, you will soon hold all that will remain of him whom the world could
not contain.

> Septimus Severus (d. AD 211), Roman emperor

Never yet has death been frightened away by screaming.

Tamburlaine (d. 1405)

Forty young men are carrying me off.

Augustus (d. 14 AD), Roman emperor

Go to the rising sun, for I am setting. Think more of death than of me.

Marcus Aurelius (d. AD 180), Roman emperor,
sensing his own death approaching

Dear me, I believe I am becoming a god.

Vespasian, Roman emperor (d. AD 79), as recorded by Suetonius

I do not want them to undress me...I want you to undress me.

Leon Trotsky (d. 1940), to his wife Natalia at a Mexican hospital
after receiving a fatal axe blow to his head. Stalin's assassins
had been trying to kill the dictator's arch-rival for more than a
decade. The Soviet revolutionary's words on the way to the
hospital were, "I feel here that this time they have succeeded"

Kill me! I'm just a man.

Che Guevara (d. 1967), Argentinian revolutionary who helped Castro seize
power in Cuba—the sergeant delegated to kill Che after his capture in Bolivia
by the CIA was so nervous of the legendary revolutionary that he botched the
fist attempt and shot Che in the legs. Another version has Che saying, "I know
you have come to kill me. Shoot coward, you are only going to kill a man"

I am cold, my friend.

> *John Sylvan Bailly (d. 1793), as a bystander remarked*
> *that he appeared to be trembling as he approached the scaffold*
> *and the guillotine. Bailly had been mayor of Paris at the start*
> *of the Revolution, but fell out of favor due to his pleas for*
> *calm and his defense of the Queen, Marie Antoinette*

A dying man can do nothing easy.

> *Benjamin Frankin (d. 1790), when urged by his daughter to roll*
> *over so as to make his breathing come more easily*

We will be so happy, Queenie. There are so many things happier than politics.

> *Charles Parnell (d. 1891), Irish politician. In his sleep he murmured, "The*
> *Conservative Party... Kiss me, sweet wife, and I will try to sleep a little"*

Water.

> *Ulysses Simpson Grant (d. 1885), eighteenth president of the United States.*
> *His last word was to his son, who had asked him if he needed anything*

Don't let it end like this. Tell them I said something.

> *Pancho Villa (d. 1923), after his assassination, the dying Mexican*
> *revolutionary was mortified to be at a loss for last words*

Oh God.

> *Mahatma ("Great Soul") Gandhi (d. 1948),*
> *Indian leader, as he was assassinated*

They won't think anything of it.

Abraham Lincoln (d. 1865), before he was assassinated by John Wilkes
Booth. He was speaking to his wife, who had wondered aloud what the
others in their party would think of their holding hands in a theater

Oh do not cry. Be good children, and we shall meet in Heaven.

Dying words of Andrew Jackson (d. 1845),
seventh president of the United States

The nourishment is palatable.

Dying words of Millard Fillmore (d. 1874),
thirteenth president of the United States

I know that I am going where Lucy is.

Dying words of Rutherford B. Hayes (d.1893),
nineteenth president of the United States
(Lucy Ware Webb Hayes was his wife)

Let's cool it brothers.

Malcolm X (d. 1966), Black Muslim leader.
To his three assassins, who shot him sixteen times

No intelligent monarch arises. There is no one in the kingdom that will make me
his master. My time has come to die.

Confucius, Chinese philosopher (d. 479 BC)

I have no enemies except those of the State.

> *Cardinal Richelieu (d. 1642), chief minister under the French King Louis XIII, when asked if he pardoned all his enemies. To his niece, he said, "I beg you to retire. Do not allow yourself to suffer the pain of seeing me dead"*

Before they put me to sleep, if I do not wake—Viva Perón!

> *Eva Perón, Argentinian populist leader (d. 1952)*

This is a mortal wound, doctor.

> *Alexander Hamilton, US Founding Father*

'Tis well.

> *General George Washington (d. 1799), first US president. Also reported, somewhat more stoically, as "I die hard but am not afraid to go"*

To the strongest!

> *Alexander the Great (d. 323 BC), when asked to whom he would leave his throne*

Oh, I am so bored with it all.

> *Winston Churchill (d. 1965), British Prime Minister, before slipping into a coma. He died nine days later*

The South! The poor South! God knows what will become of her.

> *John C. Calhoun (d. 1850), senator and champion of the Southern cause*

Let us go—let us go—these people don't want us in this land! Let us go, boys—
　take my luggage on board this frigate.

> *Simón Bolivár (d. 1830), "The Great Liberator" of*
> *Latin America, as he lay dying in Colombia*

I can't see what's happening now. My eyeglasses, where are my eyeglasses?

> *Louis Barthou (d. 1934), French politician,*
> *assassinated with King Alexander I of Yugoslavia*

Texas recognized! Archer told me so. Did you see it in the papers?

> *Stephen F. Austin (d. 1836), founder of the brand new republic of*
> *Texas—and for whom the state's chief city is named*

Do you think I have played my part pretty well through the farce of life?

> *Caesar Augustus (d. AD 14), to his friends. To his wife, he said*
> *"Live mindful of our wedlock, Livia—and farewell"*

You must not pity me in this last turn of fate. You should rather be happy in the
　remembrance of our love and in the recollection that, of all men, I was once
　the most powerful and now, at the end, have fallen not dishonorably—a
　Roman by a Roman vanquished.

> *Mark Antony (d. 30 BC), having inflicted his own, fatal blow,*
> *rather than be killed by the enemy following his defeat by*
> *Octavius at Actium. He addressed these words to Cleopatra*

Thank you, my child.

> *Count Otto Von Bismarck (d. 1898), German statesman*
> *nicknamed "The Iron Chancellor." He was speaking to his*
> *daughter, who had mopped his brow*

Whatever the result may be, I shall carry to my grave the consciousness that I at least meant well for my country.

> *James Buchanan (d. 1868),*
> *fifteenth president of the United States*

Thomas Jefferson still survives.

> *Dying words of John Adams, the longest-lived of all the*
> *US presidents, who died on July 4, 1826, at the age of 90,*
> *unaware that his supposed successor as president had died*
> *a few hours earlier at his home at Monticello in Virginia*

Is it the Fourth?

> *Thomas Jefferson (d. 1826), who died on Independence Day (and*
> *within hours of his friend John Adams)—he had signed the*
> *Declaration of Independence exactly 50 years earlier*

Italy is made—all is safe!

> *Camillo Cavour (d. 1861), Italian patriot*

I wish to be buried standing—facing Germany.

> *Georges Clemenceau (d. 1929), French President*

God bless our American institutions. They grow better by the day.

Samuel Gompers (d. 1924), labor activist

I wonder why he shot me?

*Huey P. Long (d. 1935), governor of Louisiana,
receiving a fatal bullet from an assassin's gun*

We are all going, we are all going, we are all going...oh dear.

*William McKinley (d. 1901), 25th president of the United States—he was
assassinated in Buffalo, New York, by Leon Czolgosz. "Be easy with him
boys," he had called as his assailant was wrestled to the ground*

But...but... Mr Colonel...

*Benito Mussolini (d. 1945), Italian Fascist dictator ("Il Duce"), who was
shot at the end of World War II. He was speaking to "Colonel Valerio,"
the partisan officer whose swiftly convened court condemned the
dictator to death, and was no doubt trying to talk him out of firing*

Oh look! See how the cherry blossoms fall beautifully.

Hideko Tojo (d. 1948), Japanese soldier and politician

I am going. Perhaps it is for the best.

John Tyler (d. 1862), tenth president of the United States

I do not enter any interior matters. It is so easy to write, but to write honestly is
    nearly impossible.

> *William Ewart Gladstone (d. 1898),*
> *British Prime Minister, in his last diary entry*

Young man, keep your record clean.

> *John Gough (d. 1886), American lawyer and temperance campaigner*

Ah, a road accident...a road accident.

> *Paul Doumer (d. 1932), French President, assassinated*
> *by a gunman and not, as he thought, struck by a car*

I have taken care of everything in the course of my life, only not for death—and
    now I have to die completely unprepared.

> *Cesare Borgia (d. 1507), member of the powerful*
> *(sometimes infamous) Florentine family*

I love you Sarah. For all eternity, I love you.

> *James K. Polk (d. 1849), eleventh president*
> *of the United States, spoken to his wife*

I have a terrific headache.

> *Franklin Delano Roosevelt (d. 1945), thirty-second president of*
> *the United States. He died of a cerebral hemorrhage*

Put out the light.

> *Theodore Roosevelt (d. 1919), twenty-sixth*
> *president of the United States*

France—Army—Head of the Army—Josephine.

> *Napoleon Bonaparte (d. 1821), as he lay on his deathbed in exile*
> *on the South Atlantic island of St Helena; the disjointed*
> *utterances reveal his chief, and enduring, preoccupations*

Bonaparte...the island of Elba...the King of Rome.

> *The Empress Josephine Bonaparte (d. 1814), who was divorced*
> *by the Emperor Napoleon for her failure to produce an heir for*
> *him. Her last words reveal her enduring preoccupations. Earlier,*
> *she said, "I can say with truth to all at my last moments that the*
> *first wife of Napoleon never caused a tear to flow"*

Sanson, you will show my head to the people. It is worth seeing.

> *Georges Jacques Danton (d. 1794),*
> *French revolutionary leader, to his executioner, Sanson*

Oh, my country! How I love my country!

> *William Pitt the Younger, British statesman (d. 1806). Another*
> *version has the still-youthful Prime Minister (he died at the age*
> *of 47) declaring "I think I could eat one of Bellamy's veal pies"*

No, it is better not. She will only ask me to take a message to Albert.

> *Benjamin Disraeli (d. 1881), British Conservative leader,*
> *Prime Minister, and novelist, declining an offer of a visit from*
> *Queen Victoria as he lay on his deathbed. His last recorded*
> *words were, "I had rather live, but I am not afraid to die"*

This is the last of earth. I am content.

> *John Quincy Adams (d. 1848), sixth president of the*
> *United States who died peacefully on February 23, 1848*

I do not have to forgive my enemies. I have had them all shot.

> *Ramón Maria Narváez (1800–68), Spanish general and political leader, when*
> *asked by a priest on his deathbed whether he forgave his enemies*

It is not my design to drink or to sleep, but my design is to make what haste I
can to be gone.

> *Oliver Cromwell (d. 1658), who made himself Lord Protector of England*
> *following the English Civil War and the execution of Charles I*

Ay, ay, ay, ay!

> *Rafael Trujillo (d. 1961), Dominican Republic dictator*
> *on his assassination by machine-gun fire*

Ben, make sure you play "Precious Lord, Take My Hand." Play it real pretty...
   for me.

> *Last words of Martin Luther King (d. 1969), to Ben*
> *Branch—moments later, he was shot dead*

Why? Is Garcia going on a trip?

> *General Franco (d. 1975), Spain's fascist dictator, when told*
> *that General Garcia wished to say goodbye to him*

Kitty, that is the death rattle.

> *Thomas Hart Benton (d. 1858), American senator,*
> *to his nurse who had put her ear to his wheezing chest*

Good morning, Robert.

> *Calvin Coolidge (d. 1933), twenty-ninth president*
> *of the United States. He was addressing his handyman*
> *and then shortly afterward, his wife found him*
> *lying dead on the bathroom floor*

I am ready.

> *Woodrow Wilson (d. 1924), twenty-eighth*
> *president of the United States*

Hercules! How cold is your bath.

> *Jugurtha (d. 104 BC), King of Numidia, as he was thrown into a*
> *Roman dungeon to starve to death*

I've always loved my wife, my children, and my grandchildren, and I've always
loved my country. I want to go. God, take me.

> *Dwight D. Eisenhower (d. 1969),*
> *thirty-fourth president of the United States and military hero*

They shall all be guillotined.

> *Jean-Paul Marat (d. 1793) was one of the most radical and bloodthirsty*
> *leaders of the French Revolution. On July 13, a woman named Charlotte*
> *Corday asked the guard at his apartment door if she could deliver*
> *information about a counter-revolutionary group to Marat. Marat granted*
> *her entry to his apartment where he was in the bathtub. After reading the*
> *list, he remarked, "They shall all be guillotined." As he did, Corday pulled*
> *out a knife and killed him; she had actually come to avenge the execution*
> *of a friend. Charlotte Corday was caught and executed four days later.*

Nothing more than a change of mind, my dear.

> *Dying words of James Madison (d. 1836), fourth President*
> *of the United States responding to the question "What is*
> *the matter, Uncle James?" from one of his nieces*

I want to live because there are a few things I want to do.

> *Aneurin Bevan (d. 1960), British politician, during his final illness*

I have tried so hard to do right.

> *Grover Cleveland (d. 1908), twenty-second and twenty-fourth*
> *president of the United States*

Approaching dissolution brings relief.

> *Neville Chamberlain (d. 1940), British prime minister at*
> *the start of the Second World War*

Famous Last Stands— Military Men

Soldiers, you are going to undertake a conquest of which the effects upon civilization, and the entire business of the world, are incalculable... You will give to England the most certain death stroke... We shall succeed in our enterprises. The fates are with us.

> *Napoleon, addressing his troops before the Battle of Waterloo, which would lead to defeat, and the Emperor's downfall and exile*

My center collapses, my right recedes, situation excellent. I attack!

> *Marshal Ferdinand Foch to General Joffre during the second battle of the Marne, in World War I*

Old soldiers never die. They just fade away. And like the old soldier of that ballad, I now close my military career and just fade away—an old soldier who tried to do his duty as God gave him the light to see that duty. Goodbye.

> *Snippet from the last speech of General Douglas MacArthur, relieved of his post as commander of UN forces in Korea after a very public falling out with President Truman in April 1951*

Dieu et mon droit!

> *The war cry supposedly used at the Battle of Crécy in 1346 at the*
> *start of the Hundred Years War between England and France—*
> *the English royal motto ("God and my right") in this instance referring*
> *to the right of the English rulers to the throne of France; a throne*
> *they did not succeed in gaining during this disastrous battle*

Remember the Alamo!

> *Battle cry of the Mexican revolution in honor of the 200 Texan citizen-*
> *soldiers who defended the Alamo garrison in San Antonio from February*
> *23 to March 6, 1836 and sacrificed their lives for the Republic of Texas*

Let me die in my old uniform. God forgive me for ever putting on any other!

> *Benedict Arnold (d. 1801), American soldier who sided*
> *with the losers in the War of American Independence*

Out! Out! God Almighty! Holy Cross!

> *Final battle cries of Harold Godwinson, King of England,*
> *killed at the Battle of Hastings in 1066*

The Guard dies but never surrenders!

> *Major General Pierre Cambronne, refusing to give in to a*
> *British call to surrender at the Battle of Waterloo, 1815. In the end,*
> *he had to. His final words in 1842 were "Ah, mademoiselle!*
> *Man is thought to be something, but he is nothing"*

I have sustained a continual bombardment and cannonade for twenty-four hours and have not lost a man. The enemy has demanded surrender at discretion; otherwise, the garrison is to be put to the sword, if the fort is taken. I have answered the demand with a cannon shot, and our flag still waves proudly over the wall. I shall never surrender or retreat.

Part of the famous letter from William Travis, commander of the Alamo, dated February 24, 1836, in which he appealed for help. His men were slaughtered by General Santa Anna

We've caught them napping!

Possibly the last words of General Custer at the Battle of the Little Big Horn, 1876, although no one knows for sure, as not one of his men survived. When he uttered these words, Custer was standing on a ridge overlooking the Sioux camp

Give them the cold steel, men!

Lewis Addison Armistead (d. 1863), Confederate general, l eading the charge of the Union artillery on foot with his men; he was referring to their swords, his horse having been shot out from under him, and all ammunition now spent

Well, let's forget about it and play High Five. I wish Johnny would come.

Buffalo Bill Cody (d. 1917), Western hero

God, God, won't somebody give me some more cartridges for a last shot...

> *Ike Clanton (d. 1881), rancher, shot by the Earp*
> *brothers at the Gunfight at the OK Corral*

What a pity it is that we can die but once to serve our country.

> *Nathan Hale (d. 1776), US nationalist,*
> *hanged as a spy by the British*

Texas, Texas...Margaret.

> *Sam Houston (d. 1863), Texas patriot. Margaret was*
> *his wife—he had been married to her since 1840*

I had a letter this morning from a madman who announces that he is a messenger from the Lord and will deliver his message to me tomorrow morning. We shall see.

> From a last letter written by Arthur Wellesley,
> Duke of Wellington (d. 1852)

Do you know where the apothecary lives? Then send and let him know that I should like to see him. I don't quite feel well and I will lie still till he comes..

> *Duke of Wellington (d. 1852), great military hero and architect of*
> *Napoleon's downfall at the Battle of Waterloo in 1815*

Don't give up the ship!

> *Captain James Lawrence (d. 1813), American sailor and commander of the USS* Chesapeake *against HMS* Shannon

Go one of you, my lads, with all speed to Colonel Burton, and tell him to march Webb's regiment down to the St. Charles River and cut off the retreat of the fugitives from the bridge. Now, God be praised, I die happy.

> *General James Wolfe (d. 1759), British military leader, died in Canada*

I did not mean to be killed today.

> *Vicomte de Turenne (d. 1675), French military leader, killed at the Battle of Salzback*

Captain, I must do something for my country. What shall I do?

> *Arthur Buckminster Fuller (d. 1862), Union chaplain killed at the Battle of Fredericksburg, taking a musket and presenting himself to his captain*

Now all is over. Let the piper play *Return No More*

> *Rob Roy MacCregor (d. 1734), Scottish outlaw and hero*

A little while and I will be gone from among you. Whither I cannot tell. From nowhere we come, into nowhere we go. What is life? It is the flash of a firefly in the light. It is the breath of the buffalo in the wintertime. It is as the little shadow that runs across the grass and loses itself in the sunset.

> *Isapwo Muksika Crowfoot (d. 1890), Indian chief*

Strike the tent!

> *Robert E. Lee (d. 1879), Confederate commander in the American Civil War*

We will have them, North and South. The colored people, yes, we will have
them. We must have charity, charity, charity...

> *Rear Admiral Andrew Hull Foote (d. 1863) of the US Navy*

Go ahead boys, I'm all right.

> *Lieutenant Aloysius Schmitt (d. 1941), US Navy chaplain,*
> *and the last to leave USS Oklahoma, which had been*
> *bombed by Japanese planes in Pearl Harbor*

Take a step forward, lads. It will be easier that way.

> *Erskine Childers, British-born author (of The Riddle in the Sands) and Irish*
> *patriot, as he stood before the firing squad, November 24, 1922*

Father, it is no use to depend on me. I am going to die.

> *Crazy Horse (d. 1877), famous leader of the Oglala tribe in Dakota,*
> *after being bayoneted by US soldiers following his (tricked)*
> *surrender at Camp Robinson, Nebraska. A year earlier, with*
> *Sitting Bull, he had defeated a US battalion under General Custer*

Nonsense, they couldn't hit an elephant at this dist—.

> *John Sedgwick (d. 1864), US general. In response to being advised not to put his head above the parapet during the Battle of the Wilderness*

Rejoice, we are victorious!

> *Pheidippides (d. 490 BC), uttering the words after the Battle of Marathon. Legend has it that he ran 26 miles to Athens to bring the good news, whereupon he collapsed and died. The Olympic race is named after his heroic endeavor*

Kiss me, Hardy... Now I am satisfied.

> *"Thank God, I have done my duty"... Dying words of Horatio, Lord Nelson (d. 1805), mortally wounded at the Battle of Trafalgar. He was speaking to his fellow officer, Captain Thomas Hardy— though it has been suggested he actually said "Kismet," meaning "it is Fate." A moment later, he said "God Bless you, Hardy."*

Let us cross over the river and rest under the shade of the trees.

> *Thomas J. "Stonewall" Jackson (d. 1863), who died as a result of bullets fired by his own men during the Battle of Chancellorsville during the American Civil War*

Oh my Lord Jesus! Son of God! Bless these our arms and this day's battle for
thine own glory and holy name's sake.

> *Gustavus Adolphus of Sweden (d. 1632), praying*
> *before the Battle of Lützen, in which he wore no armor*
> *(for "God was his harness") and received a mortal wound*

O Liberty, O Liberty! What crimes are committed in thy name!

> *Mme Roland (d. 1793) French intellectual politician, before*
> *being guillotined during the French Revolution*

I am mortally wounded, I think.

> *Last words of US naval hero Stephen Decatur (d. 1820), killed in a duel*

Sergeant, the Spanish bullet isn't made that will kill me.

> *William O'Neill, one of Teddy Roosevelt's Rough Riders during the*
> *Spanish–American War. Moments later he was killed by a stray bullet*

It is unbelievable.

> *Last words of Mata Hari (Gertrude Margaret Zelle), spy*
> *and femme fatale, moments before her execution by a firing*
> *squad on October 15, 1917. Earlier she told a nun, "Death is*
> *nothing, nor life either, for that matter. To die, to sleep, to pass*
> *into nothingness, what does it matter? Everything is an illusion"*

I am sorry for the mistake, but this is the first time that I've been beheaded.

> *Alexander Blackwell (d. 1747), English adventurer, about to be*
> *executed—he had laid his head on the wrong side of the block*

Steady, boys, steady!

> *Colonel Charles Dreux (d. 1861), the first Confederate*
> *field officer to be killed in battle at Newport News. Dreux's*
> *(1st) Batallion were composed of the first five companies*
> *that volunteered from Louisiana. He died while on a failed*
> *mission to capture Union officers breakfasting at Smith's Farm*

The old duffer—he broke me on the hand.

> *James Butler "Wild Bill" Hickok (d. 1876), one of*
> *Custer's scouts, who was shot dead during a game of*
> *poker in the "outlaw town" of Deadwood, South Dakota*

Give me 80 men and I'll ride through the whole Sioux nation.

> *In November 1866, Captain William J. Fetterman reported*
> *in to the 18th U.S. Infantry at Fort Phil Kearney. At the time,*
> *the regiment was tasked with containing Red Cloud and his*
> *band of Sioux. Fetterman, although inexperienced in Indian*
> *warfare, demanded an assignment. A second patrol sent*
> *out later in the day found the bodies of Fetterman and all*
> *80 of his men stripped of their clothing and horribly mutilated*

Let not my end disarm you, and on no account weep or keen for me, let the
enemy be warned of my death.

> *Genghis Khan (d. 1227) who fell ill as his forces*
> *approached the Tangut capital of Ningxia. Following*
> *the Khan's death, the Mongol army defeated the Tanguts,*
> *sacked Ningxia, and massacred all of its inhabitants*

Great God! Have I missed him?

> *Charles Dickinson (d. 1806)—just before being mortally wounded*
> *in a duel with Andrew "old hickory" Jackson. Dickinson*
> *had in fact wounded the future US president, but Jackson,*
> *wearing a voluminous coat, gave no indication that he'd been hit*

Going, Going, Gone...

I am just going outside and I may be some time.

> *Captain Lawrence ('Titus') Oates, on the ill-fated Antarctic*
> *expedition led by Captain R.F. Scott; he was sacrificing his own*
> *chance of survival to boost those of the other survivors, reduced to*
> *meager rations. Scott wrote: "We knew that poor Oates was walking*
> *to his death, but though we tried to dissuade him, we knew it was the*
> *act of a brave man and an English gentleman. We all hope to meet*
> *the end with a similar spirit, and assuredly the end is not far." Oates's*
> *Antarctic epitaph was "Hereabouts died a very gallant gentleman"*

Then puddle it, puddle it, and puddle it again.

> *James Brindley (d. 1772), engineer, while instructing*
> *his workers engaged in building a canal*

Well, children, doctor. I trust on this occasion I have said nothing unworthy of
Daniel Webster. Life, death; death, death. How curious it is.

> *Daniel Webster (d. 1852), American lawyer and politician*

It's all over now.

> *Samuel Colt (d. 1862), arms manufacturer and inventor of the Colt 45*

That will be all; now I think I'll go to sleep.

> *Henry Clay Frick (d. 1919), American industrialist*

Let me go!

> *Captain E.J. Smith (d. 1912), captain of the* Titanic, *which sank after it had*
> *struck an iceberg in 1912; he refused to climb into a lifeboat*

Stop. Go out of the room... I am about to die.

> *George Fordyce (d. 1802), Scottish physician and lecturer on*
> *medicine, addressing his daughter, who had been reading to him*

I am in some pain...my hearing and speech are very poor.

> *J. Robert Oppenheimer (d. 1967), the "Father of the A-bomb,"*
> *in a note written a few days before he died*

I don't want it.

> *Marie Curie (d. 1934), with her husband Pierre, co-discoverer of*
> *radium—she had been offered an injection to ease the pain*

From my present sensations I should say that I were dying and I am glad of it.

> *George Combe (d. 1862), phrenologist*

It is very beautiful over there.

> *Thomas Edison (d. 1931), US inventor of electric lighting*
> *and the phonograph. The words were addressed to his wife*
> *Mina, and may have referred to the view from his window*

Too many cigars this evening, I guess.

> *E.W. Scripps (d. 1926), American publisher*

Don't cut the ham too thin!

> *Last words of railroad restaurateur Fred Harvey, whose latest advertising*
> *slogan (on the Santa Fe route) had been "Meals by Fred Harvey"*

Leave the shower curtain on the inside of the tub.

> *Conrad N. Hilton, founder of the famous Hilton hotel chain*

That is false. I always have served my king loyally and sought to add to
his domain.

> *Vasco Nunez de Balbao (d. 1517), discoverer of the*
> *Pacific Ocean; he was beheaded on trumped-up charges*

I'll take a wee drop of that. I don't think there's much fear of me learning to
drink now.

> *James Cross (d. 1890), Scottish physicist (The life-long teetotaler*
> *saw no harm in a drop of the hard stuff on his deathbed)*

Courage, my lads! We are as near to heaven by sea as by land.

> *Sir Humphrey Gilbert (d. 1583), English navigator who was also*
> *Sir Walter Raleigh's half-brother (Gilbert was trying to lift the*
> *spirits of his crew as their ship the* Squirrel *went down)*

One day when the going is tough and a big game is hanging in the balance, ask the team to win one for the Gipper. I don't know where I'll be, Rock, but I'll know about it, and I'll be happy.

> *George Gipp (d. 1920), American football great*
> *("Rock" was his coach, Knute Rockne)*

No.

> *Alexander Graham Bell (d. 1922), to his wife,*
> *who had asked him not to leave her*

Tomorrow, I shall no longer be here.

> *Nostradamus (d. 1566), French soothsayer*

Well, if this is dying, there is nothing unpleasant about it.

> *Maria Mitchell (d. 1889), the first woman*
> *professor of astronomy in the United States*

Is this dying? Is this all? Is this all I feared when I prayed against a hard death?
Oh, hear this! I can bear it! I am going to where all tears will be wiped from
my eyes.

Cotton Mather (d. 1728), American-English writer

My exit is the result of too many entrées.

Deathbed utterance of Richard Monkton Milnes (d. 1885),
Victorian philanthropist, bon viveur, and politician

Stand away, fellow, from my diagram!

Archimedes (d. 212 BC), when approached by a Roman
soldier whose army had just seized the city of Syracuse; he
was drawing figures in the sand and was killed on the spot

Now I am dying. The artery ceases to beat.

Albrecht von Haller (d. 1777), physician,
as he checked his own weakening pulse

Dying is different from what I thought.

Christian Jacob Kraus (d. 1832), German professor of political science

What we know is not much. What we do not know is immense.

Pierre Laplace (d. 1827), French astronomer

And now I am officially dead.

> *Abram S. Hewitt (d. 1903), industrialist and politician,*
> *removing the oxygen mask from his face*

Nurse, it was I who discovered that leeches have red blood.

> *Baron Georges Cuvier (d. 1832), French zoologist, to his attendant*
> *who was making to apply leeches in order to bleed him*

I believe we must adjourn the meeting to some other place.

> *Adam Smith (d. 1790), Scottish economist*

I have perfect faith.

> *Count Ferdinand von Zeppelin (d. 1917),*
> *inventor of the airship that bore his name*

Don't baby me so!

> *John Pierpoint Morgan (d. 1913), business magnate*
> *and founder of the U.S. Steel Corporation*

That was the right prayer.

> *Jay Cooke (d. 1905), American banker,*
> *on overhearing a prayer for the dead*

I am not the least afraid to die.

> *Charles Darwin (d. 1882), author of*
> The Origin of Species *and founder of the theory of evolution*

I'm going over the valley.

> *Babe Ruth (d. 1948), baseball legend, when asked by*
> *a doctor where he was going. Ruth was wandering about*
> *in his hospital room, and died a short time later*

Oh God, here I go!

> *Max Baer (d. 1959), one time World Heavyweight Boxing*
> *champion; the words were uttered after a fatal heart attack*

I die.

> *Leonard Euler (d. 1783), Swiss mathematician and hugely*
> *prolific writer. He was playing with his grandson when he*
> *thus announced his death; his latest project had been*
> *calculating the orbit of the newly discovered planet Uranus*

I hope so.

> *Andrew Carnegie (d. 1919), steel magnate and*
> *philanthropist, to his wife who had bid him goodnight*

Four o'clock. How strange. So that is time. Strange. Enough!

> *Sir Henry Stanley (d. 1904), British explorer*

Goodbye, doctor. Adios, compadre!

> *Kit Carson (d. 1868), frontiersman, hunter, and trapper.*
> *He died grasping the hand of his friend, Mr. Scheurich*

Higher! Always higher.

> *Peruvian aviator Charles Chavez (d. 1910), whose plane*
> *crashed during a flying competition. He lay, suffering*
> *appalling injuries semiconscious and delirious for*
> *days, occasionally muttering, "Arriba. Siempre arriba"*

Except taxes.

> *Elisa Bonaparte (d. 1820), sister of the French Emperor Napoleon*
> *Bonaparte, on being told nothing was certain apart from death*

But I have to. So little done. So much to do!

> *Alexander Graham Bell (d. 1922), inventor of the telephone,*
> *when he was asked not to dictate so quickly from his deathbed.*
> *Even in 1922 he was busy patenting airplane designs*

My name and memory I leave to man's charitable speeches, to foreign nations,
and to the next age.

> *Francis Bacon (d. 1626), Renaissance scientist and "universal*
> *man." These words were attested to by a number of sources, who*
> *stated that he uttered them after dictating a lengthy letter, which*
> *survives. Bacon had caught pneumonia while stuffing a chicken*
> *with snow to observe the effects of refrigeration on the meat*

I am very sensible of the attachment you show me, and I hasten to thank you for it, as I feel I am now come to my last illness.

> *James Watt (d. 1819), Scottish scientist who refined the design of Newcomen's steam engine and thus speeded up the pace of change during the Industrial Revolution in Britain. He was speaking to his friends, who had gathered at his bedside*

I now feel that I am dying. Our care must be to minimize pain. Do not let the servants come into the room and keep away the youths. It will be distressing to them and they can be of no service.

> *Jeremy Bentham (d. 1832), English political theorist*

Lot of damn foolery!

> *Oliver Wendell Holmes (d. 1935), jurist, on seeing an oxygen tent going up around him*

I got four things to live by: don't say nothin' that will hurt anybody; don't give advice—nobody will take it anyway; don't complain; don't explain.

> *Edward "Death Valley Scotty" Scott (d. 1954), recluse*

We have been together for 40 years, and we will not separate now.

> *Mrs. Isadore Straus (d. 1912), passenger on the* Titanic. *She refused to take a lifeboat which would have meant separating from her husband*

KHAQQ calling Itasca [a coastguard cutter]. We must be on you, but we cannot
see you. Gas is running low.

> *Amelia Earhart (d. 1937), the first woman to fly solo*
> *across the Atlantic Ocean; her plane disappeared near the*
> *Equator after taking off from New Guinea, in the Pacific*

Fool! Not to see that our heads must in a few seconds meet in that basket.

> *George Jacques Danton (d. 1794), when forbidden to embrace*
> *his fellow sufferers prior to his execution at the scaffold*

Goodbye Cruel World

All fled all done, so lift me on the pyre; the feast is over, and the lamps expire.

> *Robert E. Howard (d. 1936); the suicide note by the*
> *creator of* Conan the Barbarian, *someone who was*
> *considerably more sensitive than his fictional hero*

To Harald, may God forgive you and forgive me too but I prefer to take my
life away and our baby's before I bring him with shame, shame of killing
him, Lupe.

> *Suicide note left by Lupe Velez (d. 1944), Hollywood actress*

The future is just old age and illness and pain...I must have peace and this is the
only way.

> *Suicide note left by James Whale (d. 1957),*
> *Hollywood director; his life was the subject of the*
> *movie* Gods and Monsters, *which starred Ian McKellen*

They tried to get me. I got them first!

> *Suicide note left by the poet Vachel Lindsay (d. 1931),*
> *who took the Lysol-drinking way out*

I must end it. There's no hope left. I'll be at peace. No one had anything to do
with this. My decision totally.

> *Suicide note left by Freddie Prinze (d. 1977), comedian*

Dear world, I am leaving you because I am bored. I feel I have lived long enough.
I am leaving you with your worries in this sweet cesspool—good luck.

> *Suicide note left by George Sanders aged 66 (d. 1972),*
> *British actor often cast as the suave villain*

We are killing ourselves because we are too happy...we do not need money, for
we are worth over 30,000 francs. We have good health and a wonderful future
before us, but we prefer to die now because we are the happiest people in the
world. We adore each other but would rather descend into the grave together
while we are still so happy.

> *Suicide note left by newlyweds Albert and Germaine Liebaut, 1923*

I'm just going out into space to find out what it's all about; if there isn't
anything, that will be OK too.

> *Grief-stricken widow Louise T. Stanton, who disappeared*
> *in a borrowed aircraft over the Atlantic in 1933*

There is no other way to change the system and get an honest right to live.

> *Suicide note of Suhrid Ganguly, (d. 1998) aged 22 who hanged*
> *himself in Calcutta, India, after becoming despondent at*
> *attempts to have his telephone fixed without paying a bribe*

I paint as a means to make life bearable. Don't weep. What I have done is best for all of us. No use, I shall never be rid of this depression.

> *Note left by the Dutch painter Vincent van Gogh, before he killed*
> *himself in Auvers sur Oise, France in 1890, aged only 37*

Here, ruining people is considered sport.

> *Vincent Foster, U.S. attorney in a note left*
> *before his apparent suicide in 1993*

Absolutely no reason except I have a toothache.

> *Suicide note left by one John Thomas D. before he jumped off the*
> *Golden Gate Bridge. Quoted in* Or Not to Be *by Marc Etkind*

I fought against the looting of the people. I have fought bare-breasted. The hatred, infamy, and calumny did not crush my spirit. I gave you my life! Now I present my death. Nothing remains. Serenely, I take the first step on the road to eternity and I leave life to enter history.

> *Getullio Vargas (d. 1954), President of Brazil, who committed suicide*

I have taken my life in order to provide capital for you...I have made the only decision I can. It's purely a business decision.

Suicide note left by one Alex C., who killed himself so his wife could collect the insurance and settle a dispute with the I.R.S. Quoted in Or Not to Be *by Marc Etkind*

I cannot face life without Arthur.

Words scribbled by Cynthia Koestler at the end of the suicide note left by her husband, Hungarian author Arthur Koestler (d. 1983). The couple had taken an overdose of barbiturates (Koestler was dying of leukemia and had written his own suicide note some months previously)

Thank you all from the pit of my burning, nauseous stomach for your letters and concern during the last years. I'm too much of an erratic, moody person! I don't have the passion anymore, and so remember, it's better to burn out than to fade away. Peace, love empathy.

Suicide note left by Kurt Cobain (d. 1994) of influential grunge band Nirvana

Goodbye everybody!

Hart Crane (d. 1932), the poet who famously killed himself by jumping overboard from the steamship Orizaba

What is the time?

Barney Barnato (d. 1897), English-born comic who became a millionaire and diamond king in South Africa, said just as he was about to jump overboard from a ship

And so I leave this world, where the heart must either break or turn to lead.

Suicide note left by the French writer Nicolas-Sebastien Chamfort (d. 1794)

To my friends: My work is done. Why wait? G.E.

Suicide note left by George Eastman (d. 1932), inventor and founder of the Eastman Kodak Company

When I am dead, and over me bright April
Shakes out her rain drenched hair,
Tho you should lean above me broken hearted,
I shall not care.
For I shall have peace.
As leafey trees are peaceful
When rain bends down the bough.
And I shall be more silent and cold hearted
Than you are now.

Suitably poetic suicide note left by poetess Sara Teasdale (d. 1933), who killed herself in her bath

Watch out please.

Last words of Egon Friedell (d. 1938), renowned Viennese author and critic and a vocal opponent of the Nazi annexation of Austria, before jumping to his death from a window to avoid capture by the Gestapo

Dearest, I feel certain that I'm going mad again. I feel we can't go through
another of those terrible times. And I shan't recover this time. I begin to hear
voices and I can't concentrate. So I'm doing what seems the best thing to do...
I don't think two people could have been happier than we have been. V.

Suicide note left on the mantelpiece of their Sussex home by the
English writer Virginia Woolf (d. 1941) for her husband Leonard. She
had then filled her pockets with stones and waded into the River Ouse

At this moment I wish I were dead. I just can't cope any more.

Suicide note attributed to Ian Curtis (d. 1980) founder of British
rock group Joy Division. Curtis died on the eve of a tour to
America, the rest of the group went on to form New Order

And now, in keeping with Channel 40's policy of always bringing you the latest
in blood and guts, in living color, you're about to see another first—an
attempted suicide.

Christine Hubbock (The TV newscaster shot herself live on air on
Florida TV station WXLT-TV in 1970; she died 14 hours later)

Paetus, it doesn't hurt!

Arria, wife of Roman Emperor Caecina Paetus (d. 42 BC),
plunging a dagger into her own breast, having commanded
her husband to kill himself and he, sensible fellow, having
shown some reluctance. His wife had no such qualms

Everything disgusts me.

> *Réné Crevel (d. 1935), French surrealist poet,*
> *in his suicide note ("Je suis dégoûté de tout")*

Woe to the mother, in her close of day,

Woe to her desolate heart, and temples gray,

When she shall hear

Her loved one's story whispered in her ear:

'Woe, woe!' Will be the cry,—

No quiet murmur like the tremulous wail—

> *Words written by James V. Forrestal (d. 1949),*
> *US Secretary of Defense, before committing suicide*

One day you'll read about it. Phil Ochs—A Suicide at 35.

> *Message from Phil Ochs (d. 1976) given out at his last concert*

Stay back, this could hurt someone.

> *R. Budd Dwyer (d. 1987), former State Treasurer for the*
> *Commonwealth of Pennsylvania, while brandishing the pistol*
> *with which he shot himself seconds later in front of an assembled*
> *crowd with TV cameras rolling. (He was due to be sentenced to a*
> *hefty prison term for bribery and conspiracy the following day)*

I am a nuisance.

> *Suicide note left for his wife by John Berryman (d. 1972),*
> *American poet, who drowned himself in the Mississippi*

I don't believe that people should take their own lives without deep and
thoughtful reflection over a considerable period of time.

Wendy O. Williams (d. 1998) lead singer
with punk band the Plasmatics

We had a death pact. I have to keep my half of the bargain. Please bury me next
to my baby. Bury me in my leather jacket, jeans and motor cycle boots.
Goodbyee.

Sid Vicious (d. 1979) bass player with legendary punk
band The Sex Pistols. High on heroin Sid had previously
stabbed girlfriend Nancy Spungen to death in 1978
following an argument. The note was found after his
cremation in the pocket of his leather jacket

Reports of My Death...
Obituaries, Early and Late

John Le Mesurier wishes it to be known that he conked out on November 15th.
He sadly misses family and friends.

> *Death announcement of John Le Mesurier (d. 1983),*
> *British actor and star of* Dad's Army

I'd rather be Frank Capra than God—if there is a Frank Capra.

> *From the obituary of Garson Kanin, American screenwriter and*
> *director, in* The Times *newspaper, March 16, 1999*

Reports of my death are greatly exaggerated.

> *Mark Twain (Samuel L. Clemens, d. 1910), US writer, on learning that his*
> *obituary had been published, in a cable to the Associated Press*

I've just read that I am dead. Don't forget to delete me from your list of
subscribers.

> *Rudyard Kipling (d. 1936), Indian-born British writer, writing to a*
> *magazine that had mistakenly published an announcement of his death*

Mr Adler brought dignity to the harmonica.

> *Snippet from* The New York Times *obituary to Larry Adler, August 7, 2001*

Well, it appears that the pipe has finally nailed me.

> *Journalist Robert Fiddes Alexander, in his self-written obituary in* The Dallas Morning News, *November 28, 1998. He ended the self-penned tribute with, "I'm sure many readers will call this self-written obit a final flight of journalistic ego. Well, let 'em. Cancer may have taken my pipe, but not my sense of humor... Please help me exit laughing during a celebrating wake at our home following the service." What a way to go*

Miss Emily Wilding Davison, the suffragist who interfered with the King's horse during the race for the Derby, died in hospital at 4.50 yesterday afternoon. She underwent an operation on Friday and had remained in a grave condition ever since.

> *Notice in* The Times, *June 9, 1913*

He was an average guy who could carry a tune.

> *Bing Crosby (d. 1977), when asked by a magazine to pen his own funeral tribute*

I carry on a lot of the functions of an adult, but I have to force myself.

> *William Steig, cartoonist (d. 2003), best known as the author of* Shrek!, *the children's story that became an Oscar-winning movie. Quoted in his obituary in the* Daily Telegraph *newspaper*

She won't be there.

> *Arthur Miller to a journalist who'd asked if he would be*
> *attending his ex-wife Marilyn Monroe's funeral (the undertone of the*
> *answer was "Why would I go?"). Stunned by her apparent suicide,*
> *Miller was unable to force himself to attend the ceremony*

An honest, faithful, and devoted follower, a trustworthy, discreet, and straightforward man, and possessed of strong sense; he filled a position of great and anxious responsibility, the duties of which he performed with such constant and unceasing care as to secure for himself the real friendship of the Queen.

> *The Official Court Circular giving news of the death of John*
> *Brown (March 27, 1883), the devoted servant of Queen Victoria*

Toothy Christian busybody and self-appointed guardian of the nation's morals Mrs. Mary Whitehouse died on 23 November 2001 at the ripe old age of 91.

> *Gay and Lesbian Humanist Association on the death of the*
> *head of the British National Viewers' and Listeners'*
> *Association (NVALA) and high-profile homophobe*

Ridiculous...the man didn't have a heart.

> *Arthur Scargill, British miners' leader, on hearing that the former National*
> *Coalboard Chairman, Sir Ian MacGregor, had died from a heart attack*

Father died terribly and with difficulty. God gives the righteous an easy death.

> *The Soviet dictator Josef Stalin's death in March 1953, as*
> *reported much later by his daughter Svetlana Alliluyeva*

It's too bad. Goodbye. It's now 6.30. The plane is rolling around and descending rapidly. I am grateful for the truly happy life I have enjoyed until now. PLEASE LORD HELP ME.

> *Note written by Hirotsugu Kawaguchi on JAL flight 123*
> *moments before it crashed in August 2002*

Wish you were here!

> *Words on cards received by the friends of Johnny Morgan,*
> *British builder, days after his cremation*

Aden, Monday—Dr. Livingstone died in June, of dysentery, at Lake Bembe, after wading through water for four days. His body has been preserved in salt by his native servants, and is proceeding to Zanzibar

> *Telegram received via Reuters news agency of the death of the famous*
> *explorer and missionary. Livingstone died on May 1, 1873, but notice of his*
> *death did not reach England until January of the following year*

If you need anything, just whistle.

> *Inscription on the gold whistle placed in the urn containing*
> *the ashes of Humphrey Bogart by his widow, Lauren Bacall.*
> *They were the words she had spoken to him in the movie*
> To Have and Have Not, *which was their first film together*

If, like Antaeus he fell, like Antaeus he rose, and declining all adventitious aid,
   relied solely on the bow string of that mighty spirit, which, if slackened for a
   moment, was as quickly re-strung...

...an inheritance as profitable as it must be endearing, and such as few fathers
   ever possessed the power of bequeathing to their children.

> The Dumfries Courier *waxing lyrical on the death of, and literary
> legacy left by, the novelist and poet Sir Walter Scott (d. 1832)*

Ours is not the grief of prostration, the grief that saps the will. It is tempered by
   rage and hatred and determination. We shall transmute it into fighting energy
   to carry on the Old Man's fight. Let us say farewell to him in a manner worthy
   of his disciples, like good soldiers of Trotsky's army. Not crouching in
   weakness and despair, but standing upright with dry eyes and clenched fists.
   With the song of struggle and victory on our lips. With the song of confidence
   in Trotsky's Fourth International, the International Party that shall be the
   human race!

> *Obituary for Leon Trotsky, read out at the Leon Trotsky Memorial
> Meeting at the Diplomat Hotel in New York City, August 28, 1940*

This morning, Captain Brown was hung. He is not Old Brown any longer; he is
   an angel of light.

> *Henry David Thoreau, writing in Massachusetts after the
> execution by hanging of John Brown in Virginia*

In our lives many of us have lived with many different pets and we loved them all... There's a lot more grieving ahead, but when I put my head on the pillow at night, I know he's looking down at me saying, "Thanks Pop, it's OK. I've met all of the pets that you loved so dearly, and we're having a good time knowing that we will all be together with you again someday. Until then, thanks, I'll get back to you later, Pop. There's a squirrel running across the clouds that I need to chase."

> *Warren Eckstein (pet and animal editor on NBC's* Today *show),*
> *paying tribute to his dear-departed dog, Rio*

I never gave away anything without wishing I had kept it; nor kept anything without wishing I had given it away.

> *American actress Louise Brooks, suggesting her own epitaph in*
> *an interview to Kenneth Tynan in* The New Yorker *in 1979*

The decease of this celebrated man was erroneously announced some years ago—but the latest St. Louis papers state that he died at Charette village, on the Missouri, on the 26th of Sept. in the ninetieth year of his age. When his death was made known to the general assembly of the new state, it was resolved that the members should wear crape on the left arm for the space of 20 days, and to adjourn for that day, in respect to his memory.

> *Notice in* Niles' Weekly Register of Baltimore, *November 4, 1820,*
> *of the death of Daniel Boone, frontiersman*

... a giant panda, Santa Claus and the Jolly Green Giant rolled into one... he wore his rotundity with dignity and grace.

Snippet from The New York Times *obituary of*
James Beard (d. 1985), cookery-book writer

[He published *The Great Gatsby*] at a time when gin was the national drink and sex was the national obsession.

Snippet from The New York Times *obituary of F. Scott Fitzgerald*
(d. 1940). The Great Gatsby *came out in 1925*

She sleeps alone at last.

Robert Benchley (d. 1945), US humorist, suggesting an epitaph for an actress

[George IV contributed more] to the demoralization of society than any prince recorded in the pages of history.

Comment by contemporary English biographer
Robert Huish on the passing of the English King in 1830

There never was an individual less regretted by his fellow creatures than this deceased King. What heart has heaved one sob of unnecessary sorrow?

Obituary for King George IV in The Times *newspaper in 1830*

The smoker's and drinker's princess.

The unofficial obituary bandied about in the British tabloid press
for HRH Princess Margaret, who died in 2002. (The late princess was
a chain smoker and known to be fond of Famous Grouse whiskey)

Here lies Robert Maxwell. He lies everywhere else.

> *Britain's satirical* Private Eye *magazine, on the late (and not much missed) media tycoon, who died in 1991. (Having presided over the greatest pension-fund misappropriation in British history)*

You helped give a shape to slipstreaming time with a wave of your hand.

> *Line from the elegy composed by the poet laureate Andrew Motion, on the death of HM Queen Elizabeth the Queen Mother in 2002*

How can they tell?

> *Dorothy Parker's comment on hearing of the death of US president Calvin Coolidge in 1933*

In affectionate remembrance
Of English cricket
Which died at the Oval,
On 29th August, 1882.
Deeply lamented by a large circle
Of sorrowing friends and acquaintances.
R.I.P.
N.B. The body will be cremated, and the ashes taken to Australia.

> *"Epitaph" penned by a group of wags and printed in the* Sporting Times *in 1882—the year an Australian team won for the first time on English soil. Hence the "Ashes," the trophy for which the two teams have competed ever since*

Where There's a Will—
Requests and Bequests

[No cross or] any instrument of torture or symbol of blood sacrifice.

Instructions left by George Bernard Shaw (d. 1950)
for his cremation, without religious ceremony

Pray for me—real loud.

One of the last, short letters—written on Christmas Eve,
1913—from Ambrose Bierce, author of the Devil's Dictionary
who "disappeared" while an observer with Pancho Villa's
rebel army during the Mexican revolution

Had we lived, I should have had a tale to tell of the hardihood, endurance and
courage of my companions, which would have stirred the hearts of every
Englishman. These rough notes and our dead bodies must tell the tale.

Diary entry of Captain Robert Falcon Scott (d. 1912) on the
doomed Antarctic expedition on which all perished

I must hasten away since my baggage has been sent off before me.

> *"La Riviere" de Bailli (d. 1605), French doctor,*
> *having disposed of all his worldly goods*

And I do hereby constitute and appoint my said loving wife my sole executrix of this my last will and testament, revoking all former wills. Witness my hand on this day.

> *Closing words of the will of the English composer Henry Purcell (d. 1695)*

It is my intention to make no provision herein for my son Christopher or my daughter Christina for reasons which are well known to them.

> *Clause from the will of Joan Crawford (d. 1977),*
> *Hollywood actress. Christina Crawford Koontz later published*
> *her book* Mommie Dearest, *on which the movie of the same name*
> *is based, detailing her mother's cruelty. Crawford was not much*
> *more generous with her two other children, for whom she placed money*
> *($75,000 each) in trust with miserly hand-outs (considering their mother's*
> *wealth) starting with the sum of $5,000 at age 30, rising to $45,000 at age 45*

Did I not say that I was writing this Requiem for myself?

> *Wolfgang Amadeus Mozart (d. 1791), referring to his* Requiem Mass,
> *the commission for which he received in 1791 and the composition*
> *of which oppressed him greatly. He died in the same year,*
> *aged only 35, and his body was thrown into a pauper's grave*

I go to God knowing at least as a comedian I was one of a kind. Shalom.

> *Concluding statement of the will of comedian Phil Silvers*
> *(d. 1985), famous for his Sergeant Bilko roles*

The worms would eat me, the ducks would eat the worms and my relatives
would eat the ducks.

> *John "Mad Jack" Fuller, member of parliament for Rose Hill*
> *(now Brightling) in Sussex in the nineteenth century. Fuller gave the*
> *above as the reason for building himself a pyramidal mausoleum*
> *in Brightling churchyard—he was afraid of being eaten by his relatives.*
> *Inside there are said to be scattered shards of glass, so that "when the*
> *devil comes to claim his own he might at least cut his feet"*

A gift of ten shillings sterling, to buy her [my wife] a pocket handkerchief to
weep after my decease.

> *An unusually thoughtful last wish and extravagance,*
> *left by a Scottish doctor in the early 1900s*

Pray let dear Lady Hamilton have my hair, and all other things belonging to me...
I wish I had not left the deck, for I shall soon be gone.

> *Last wishes of Horatio, Lord Nelson, mortally wounded at the*
> *Battle of Trafalgar in 1805, communicated to Captain Hardy*

As the world was turned topsy-turvy, it was fit that he should be so buried that he might be right at last.

> *Burial instructions, which were carried out in strict accordance with the last wishes of one Major Peter Labelliere, who was buried vertically—head downward—on Box Hill, Surrey, England, in 1800*

Alas, poor woman! She ask my pardon? I beg hers with all my heart: take back that answer.

> *The dying King Charles II (d. 1685), on hearing that his consort, Catherine of Braganza, had sent word to him that she begged his forgiveness—the King had little to forgive; it was he who had made her life a torment with his succession of mistresses*

The earth is suffocating... swear to make them cut me open, so that I won't be buried alive.

> *Frédéric Chopin (d. 1849), in his last request, written in shaky handwriting*

My black mare and sorrel horses I give to you, father. There are about 60 dollars in my pocket book. There are papers in my trunk to be turned over to the Department [Quartermaster's] to settle. Once more, goodbye, beloved father, mother, sisters, all. Ever yours.

> *George D. Bayard (d. 1862)—General Bayard— at Fredericksburg. This was the will he drew up on the battlefield where he was mortally wounded*

[My body is] to be carried to the nearest convenient burial ground accompanied
by not more than two persons without trappings.

> *Dying instructions of Florence Nightingale (d. 1910),*
> *the famous English nurse and "Lady of the Lamp" during the*
> *Crimean War. She insisted that she wanted no memorial*

Then there will be at least one man who will regret my death.

> *Phrase from the will of the German writer Heinrich Heine*
> *(d. 1856), explaining why he was leaving everything to his wife*
> *Eugenie on one condition only that she remarry*

I am ready to meet my Maker. Whether my Maker is prepared for the great
ordeal of meeting me is another matter.

> *Winston Churchill, on his 75th birthday—his last*
> *discernible words as he lay dying, to his daughter*
> *Mary Soames, were, "I'm so bored with it all"*

I hereby delete in its entirety Article Fourth of my said Last Will and Testament.
I purposely make no provision for the benefit of Tom Clark.

> *Codicil to Will (drawn up a year before the actor's death)*
> *of Rock Hudson (d. 1985) doing Clark, Hudson's former lover,*
> *out of what would have been a mighty favorable bequest*

I give and bequeath all of my personal effects and clothing to Lee Strasberg, or
if he should predecease me, then to my Executor hereinafter named, it being
my desire that he distribute these, in his sole discretion, among my friends,
colleagues and those to whom I am devoted.

Extract from the will of Marilyn Monroe (d. 1962). Strasberg was
Monroe's acting teacher, a man responsible for helping such luminaries
as Paul Newman, Al Pacino, Jane Fonda, James Dean, Dustin Hoffman,
Robert DeNiro, Jack Nicholson, and Steve McQueen among others

[Make provision for] the laud and praising of God, the health of our soul, and
somewhat to our dignity royal, but avoiding damnable pomp and outrageous
superfluities.

Funeral wishes of Henry VII (d. 1509)

If during these 80 years, the Lord Jesus Christ shall come to reign on earth, then
the Public Trustee upon obtaining proof which shall satisfy them of His
identity, shall pay to the Lord Jesus Christ all the property they hold on
His behalf.

Last wishes of Ernest Digweed, retired schoolmaster,
who died in 1976 leaving £26,000 ($44,000) in the hands of the
Public Trustees, instructed as above. (If, by 2056, Christ has not appeared
to claim His bequest, the whole amount will revert to the State)

To avoid any confusion, I leave my entire estate to the lucky person who finds this bottle, and to my attorney, Barry Cohen, share and share alike—Daisy Singer Alexander, June 20, 1937.

Message placed in a bottle by the eccentric Singer sewing machine heiress and thrown into the River Thames. It was picked up twelve years later on a beach near San Francisco by one Jack Wrum, who happened to be jobless, but, thanks to this lucky find, became a millionaire several times over

I request that no person other than my immediate family and the persons who shall prepare my remains for interment be permitted to view my remains after death has been pronounced. I further request a private funeral and that I be clothed in white and placed in a modestly priced crypt in Forest Lawn Memorial Park, Glendale, California.

Clause from the will of Carole Lombard (d. 1942), Hollywood actress, who died in a plane crash

If any person other than my son, Edward, shall claim to be a child of mine or the descendant of a child of mine... I direct my Executors to resist such claim; but if any court shall nevertheless determine that such person is a descendant of mine, I give to such person the sum of Ten Dollars ($10.00) and no more.

Clause from the will of Edward G. Robinson (d. 1973), Hollywood actor—taking no chances

In order that the vulgar may not walk about upon me.

> *Medieval French nobleman of the house of*
> *Du Châtelet, requesting burial in one of the columns*
> *in the church of Neufchâteau for the above reason*

To Baron Nicolas de Gunzburg, the Russian ikon, which is now located in my apartment in New York, New York; the sculpture of an Egyptian woman's head, which is now located in my cottage on my Buxton Hill Realty; and the book by Paul Muratoff, which was published by A La Vielle Russie and which is entitled *Thirty-Five Russian Primitives*.

> *Clause from the will of Cole Porter (d. 1964) who*
> *distributed his personal effects, "tangible personal*
> *property," with extreme care and precision*

You can keep the things of bronze and stone and give me one man to remember me just once a year.

> *Damon Runyan (d. 1946)*

Promise me you will never marry an old man again.

> *William Wycherley (d. 1715), dramatist, who died—aged 75—days*
> *after marrying a young woman, and addressing these*
> *words to his new, shortly-to-be-widowed wife*

[If Shirlee did not survive him, Fonda left his estate] to the Omaha Community
    Playhouse, at Omaha, Nebraska, to be used for such capital improvements,
    and for the maintenance and operation thereof, as the governing body of said
    Playhouse deems proper, this gift shall be known as "The Henry and Shirlee
    Fonda Bequest."

Clause from the will of Henry Fonda (d. 1982), Hollywood actor

Bury me where the birds will sing over my grave.

Alex Wilson (d. 1786), Scottish-born ornithologist

I am going to pay you the greatest compliment... I am not going to leave you
    a cent.

Lord Beaverbrook, Canadian press baron,
to his great-nephew Jonathan Aitken

Lift me up that I might die standing, not lying down like a cow.

Siward, warrior Earl of Northumberland (d. 1055)

Laissez la verdure.

George Sand (d. 1876), French writer and mistress of Chopin
(the name Sand was a pseudonym—she had been born
Amantine Aurore Dudevant). Sand wanted her grave to be
left to become overgrown by nature—"leave the greenery"

[I wish to be] embalmed and buried in the same manner in which my beloved
mother was buried upon her death, and that my grave be constructed in a
vault in the same manner as my beloved mother's last resting place was
constructed for her burial; and I also direct that I shall be buried in the grave
immediately alongside of that of my dear departed mother.

> *Burial instructions contained in the will of Harry Houdini*
> *(d. 1926), escape artist. He was keen on the idea of his*
> *spirit returning from the dead and locating the*
> *right body was an important factor*

Now squeeze this.

> *Former mayor Edward Horley (d. 1975), instructing his executors*
> *to slice a lemon in half, and send one half to the tax man*

[I leave] all my right, title and interest to my ranch, consisting of a house and
acreage located outside of Abiquiu, in the County of Rio Arriba and State of
New Mexico, which was formerly part of the "Ghost Ranch"... together with
the furnishings therein... to my friend, John Bruce Hamilton, or if he does
not survive me, to the United Presbyterian Church in the United States
of America...

> *Last will of U.S. painter Georgia O'Keefe (d. 1986).*
> *Her "friend" was a man who had turned up at her ranch,*
> *and managed to become her closest companion*

I am just going. Have me decently buried and do not let my body be put into a vault in less than two days after I am dead. Do you understand me?

Last wishes of General George Washington,
communicated verbally to Tobias Lear, his secretary

Not unmindful of my son John, I give all my estate both real and personal to my wife Grace Coolidge, in fee simple—Home at Washington, District of Columbia this twentieth day of December, nineteen hundred and twenty six.

Last will and testament of US president Calvin Coolidge (d. 1933)
in its entirety! (Perhaps only to be expected from a man of few
words such as he.) Coolidge deliberately disinherited his son

... the cheapest funeral and burial.

Burial instructions contained in the will of F. Scott Fitzgerald, in
an amendment added on November 10, 1940 just over a month
before the writer's death of a heart attack on December 21

... no play which I have written shall, for the purpose of presenting it as a first-class attraction on the English-speaking stage, be changed in any manner...

Extract from the will of Tennessee Williams (d. 1983),
keen to preserve intact his literary legacy

I commit my soul into the hands of my Saviour, in full confidence that having redeemed it and washed it in His most precious blood He will present it as faultless before the throne of my Heavenly Father; and I entreat my children to maintain and defend, at all hazard, and at any cost of personal sacrifice, the blessed doctrine of the complete atonement for sin through the blood of Jesus Christ, once offered, and through that alone.

First article of the will of John Pierpont Morgan (d. 1913), revealing, to the surprise of many, a profoundly religious private man

The meek shall inherit the earth but not the mineral rights.

J. Paul Getty, eccentric billionaire and recluse—and famously tight-fisted (he installed a pay phone at his English country pile)

"

Here Lies...
Tombstones and Epitaphs

"

A Gentle Man and a Gentleman

> *Words engraved on the tombstone of former World Heavyweight boxing champion Jack Dempsey (d. 1983, aged 97) in Southampton Cemetery, Southampton, New York*

When I am dead, I hope it may be said:
"His sins were scarlet, but his books were read."

> *Epitaph which Hilaire Belloc (d. 1953) wrote for himself in 1923, although it does not appear on his grave in West Grinstead, Sussex*

He thinketh no evil.

> *Words engraved on the tombstone of Henry Ward Beecher (d. 1887), U.S. abolitionist, in Brooklyn, New York*

Truth and History.
21 Men.
The Boy Bandit King—
He Died As He Lived.

> *Words engraved on William H. Bonney's (d. 1881) tombstone,*
> *a.k.a. "Billy the Kid," in Fort Sumner cemetery, New Mexico*

Kata ton daimona eay toy.

> *Words engraved on the tombstone of the grave of*
> *Jim Morrison (d. 1971), lead singer of The Doors, buried in the*
> *Père Lachaise Cemetery, Paris ("True to his own spirit")*

And alien tears will fill for him
Pity's long broken urn
For his mourners will be outcast men
And outcasts always mourn

> *The inscription on a sculpture at Oscar Wilde's (d. 1900) grave.*
> *Wilde shares the same Paris cemetery as Jim Morrison (above)*

A star on earth—a star in heaven.

> *Words engraved on the tombstone of singer Karen Carpenter*
> *(d. 1983), buried in Cyprus, California*

My Jesus Mercy.

> *Words engraved on the tombstone of Al (Alphonse) Capone*
> *(d. 1947), buried in Mt Carmel Cemetery, Chicago, Illinois*

And Defender of the Constitution

> *Words engraved on the tombstone of Jefferson Davis (d. 1889),*
> *president of the Confederate States of America, buried in*
> *Hollywood Cemetery, Richmond, Virginia*

The Greatest Blues Singer in the World

Will Never Stop Singing

> *Words engraved on the tombstone of Bessie Smith (d. 1937),*
> *buried in Mount Lawn Cemetery, Sharon Hill, Pennsylvania*

...that nothing's so sacred as honor and nothing's so loyal as love.

> *Words engraved on the tombstone of*
> *Wyatt Earp, buried in Colma, California*

But I tell you, my lord fool, out of this

Nettle, danger, we pluck this flower, safety.

> *Words inscribed on the tomb of New Zealand-born writer*
> *Katherine Mansfield (d. 1923) in the Protestant cemetery at Avon,*
> *Fontainebleu, in France. The words are from Shakespeare and were*
> *used on the title page of her 1920 collection of short stories, entitled* Bliss

Equity-Integrity.

> *Words engraved on the tombstone of store founder Marshall*
> *Field, (d. 1906) buried in Graceland Cemetery, Chicago, Illinois*

Vocatus Atque

Non vocatus

Deus aderit

> *Words engraved on the tombstone of Carl Jung (d. 1961),*
> *Swiss psychologist, buried in Fluntern Cemetery, Zurich,*
> *Switzerland ("Invoked or not, the god is present")*

Workers of all lands unite.

The philosophers have only

Interpreted the world in various ways;

The point is to change it.

> *Words engraved on the tombstone of Karl Marx*
> *(d. 1883), German political philosopher,*
> *buried in Highgate Cemetery, Highgate, London*

All the flowers are all made sweeter

By the sunshine and the dew,

So this old world is made brighter

By the lives of folks like you.

> *Words engraved on the tombstone of Bonnie Parker*
> *(d. 1934), buried in Crown Hill Cemetery, Dallas, Texas*

A friend to honesty and a foe to crime.

> *Words engraved on the tombstone of Allan Pinkerton (d. 1884),*
> *founder of the Pinkerton Detective Agency and forefather of the*
> *CIA, buried in Graceland Cemetery, Chicago, Illinois*

In loving memory from the Family.

> *Words engraved on the tombstone of mobster Benjamin "Bugsy" Siegel*
> *(d. 1947), buried in Hollywood Memorial Park, Hollywood, California*

That's all folks!

> *Words engraved on the tombstone of Mel Blanc*
> *(d. 1989)—the voice of Bugs Bunny—buried in Hollywood*
> *Memorial Park, Hollywood, California*

She did it the hard way.

> *Words engraved on the tombstone of Bette Davis (d. 1989),*
> *buried in Forest Lawn, Hollywood Hills, California*

Everybody Loves Somebody Sometime.

> *Words engraved on the tombstone of Dean Martin (d. 1995),*
> *buried in Westwood Memorial Cemetery, Los Angeles, California*

One of a king.

> *Words engraved on the tombstone of Buddy Rich (d. 1987),*
> *buried in Westwood Memorial Park, Westwood, California*

The evil that men do lives after them. The good is oft interred with their bones.

> *Mark Antony (d. 30 BC). From his speech at*
> *the funeral of the assassinated Julius Caesar*

I've played everything but the harp.

> *Lionel Barrymore (d. 1954), U.S. actor, when asked*
> *which words he would like inscribed on his tombstone*

This grave contains all that was mortal

of a

Young English Poet.

Who on his deathbed, in the bitterness of heart

At the malicious power of his enemies,

Desired these words to be engraven on his tombstone

"Here lies one whose name was writ in water."

Feb. 24, 1821

> *Epitaph to the poet Keats in the Protestant*
> *Cemetery in Rome, where he died*

FREE AT LAST, FREE AT LAST

THANK GOD ALMIGHTY

I'M FREE AT LAST.

> *Inscription on the grave of Martin Luther King (d. 1968),*
> *buried in South View Cemetery, Atlanta, Georgia*

Goodnight, sweet prince,

And flights of angels sing thee to thy rest.

> *Inscription on the marble tomb of Douglas Fairbanks Jr. (d. 2000), in*
> *Hollywood Cemetery (the words are from Shakespeare's* Hamlet)

Nyirmachabelli.

> *Name on the tombstone of Dian Fossey (d. 1985), naturalist—it*
> *was her Rwandan name, and means "the woman who lives alone*
> *on the mountain." Her epitaph reads: "No one loved gorillas*
> *more/Rest in peace, dear friend/Eternally protected/In this*
> *sacred ground/You are home/Where you belong"*

Here he lies where he longed to be;

Home is the sailor, home from the sea,

And the hunter home from the hill.

> *Inscription on the grave of writer Robert Louis Stevenson*
> *in Samoa, where he died in 1894*

CAROLINE OF BRUNSWICK

Born 17th May, 1768.

Died 7th August, 1821.

Aged 54.

The outraged Queen of England.

> *The inscription which Queen Caroline (d. 1821), the unfortunate*
> *wife of George IV, had penned for her coffin—needless to say, the*
> *plaque was not allowed to remain in place there after her death*

For each of us there comes a moment when death takes us by the hand and

says—it is time to rest, you are tired, lie down and sleep.

> *Will Hay (d. 1949), British comic—this was the epitaph carved on his*
> *tombstone, the words taken from a book he was reading when he died*

Shed not for her the bitter tear

Nor give the heart to vain regret.

'Tis but the casket that lies here,

The gem that fills it sparkles yet.

> *Belle Starr (d. 1889), "Bandit Queen" of the Old West,*
> *epitaph on the horse thief and bandit's gravestone*

In The Prison of His Days

Teach The Free Man How to Praise.

> *Memorial to the poet W.H. Auden (d. 1973) in Poets' Corner in Westminster*
> *Abbey, London. Auden is buried in Kirchstetten, Austria*

Nature and Nature's laws lay hid in night:

God said, "Let Newton be!" and all was light.

> *Epitaph on Sir Isaac Newton (d. 1727),*
> *composed in the eighteenth century by Alexander Pope*

So we beat on, boats against the current, borne back ceaselessly into the past.

> *Inscription on the tomb of F. Scott Fitzgerald*
> *(d. 1940) at Rockville Union Cemetery, Maryland.*
> *Fitzgerald died of a heart attack at the age of 44*

May the Divine Spirit that Animated Babe Ruth to Win the Crucial Game of Life

Inspire the Youth of America!

> *Words on the grave monument of George Herman "Babe" Ruth (d. 1948)*

Lie light upon him, earth! Tho' he

Laid many a heavy load on thee

> *Epitaph on the English architect Sir John Vanbrugh, transcribed in 1759*

John Luther Jones

1864–1900

To the memory of the locomotive engineer, whose name as "Casey Jones"

became a part of Folklore and the American language. "For I'm going to run

her till she leaves the rail—or make it on time with the southbound mail."

> *Tombstone of "Casey" Jones in Calvary Cemetery, Jackson, Tennessee*

Good frend for Iesvs sake forbeare,

To digg the dvst encloased heare!

Bleste be ye man yt spares thes stones,

And curst be he yt moves my bones.

> *Epitaph on William Shakespeare's (d. 1616) grave at*
> *Holy Trinity Church, Stratford-on-Avon, England*

Exit Burbage.

> *Epitaph to Richard Burbage (d. 1619), famous Elizabethan*
> *actor; it appeared in an early collection of epitaphs.*
> *Any writing on his tombstone disappeared long ago*

Here lies

Copenhagen

The charger ridden by

The Duke of Wellington

The entire day, at the

Battle of Waterloo

Born 1808. Died 1836.

God's humbler instrument, though meaner clay,

Should share the glory of that glorious day.

> *On the famous horse's grave at Wellington's country home,*
> *where his beloved mount was buried with full military honors*

In the beginning is my end. In my end is my beginning.

> *Line from the memorial to T.S. Eliot (d. 1965) in*
> *St Michael's Church, East Coker, Somerset, where the poet is*
> *buried. The line comes from his poem the* Four Quartets

Si monumentum quaeris, circumspice.

> *Epitaph to Sir Christopher Wren (d. 1723) in St Paul's*
> *Cathedral; his cathedral was his lasting memorial.*
> *("If you seek his monument, look around")*

1616, May 2, Rebecca Wrothe, wyff of
Thomas Wroth, gent., a Virginia lady borne,
here buried in ye chauncell.

> *Register entry in Gravesend Church, Kent, in the chancel*
> *of which Pocohontas was buried, after coming to England with*
> *her husband John Rolfe. The church burned down two centuries later*

Sleep after toyle, port after stormie seas,
Ease after warre, death after life, does greatly please.

> *Epitaph on the tomb of Polish-born novelist*
> *Joseph Conrad (d. 1924), in St Thomas's Roman*
> *Catholic Church, Canterbury, Kent, England*

Reader! I am to let thee know,
Donne's body only lies below:
For could the grave his soul comprise,
Earth would be richer than the skies.

> *Epitaph on the Reverend John Dunne (d. 1631)*
> *in St Paul's Cathedral, London*

The finder of many melodies.

> *Epitaph to the composer Rossini (d. 1868)*

Farewell, great painter of mankind,

Who reached the noblest point of art;

Whose pictured morals charmed the mind,

And, through the eye, correct the heart.

If genius fire thee, reader, stay

If nature touch thee, drop a tear:

If neither move thee, turn away,

For Hogarth's honoured dust lies here.

> *Epitaph to the painter William Hogarth (d. 1764)*
> *in Chiswick Churchyard, London—penned by Garrick*

Capt. Samuel

Jones' Leg which

was amputated

July 7 1804.

> *"Tombstone" in Washington, New Hampshire, containing*
> *the leg of Samuel Jones. Amputated limbs were occasionally*
> *given their own "resting places," while their owners lived on*

Strange is my name and I'm on strange ground

And Strange it is I can't be found.

> *Epitaph inscribed on a tree by William Strange, an early pioneer,*
> *and after whom Strange Creek, West Virginia, was named.*
> *Strange died of exposure on a surveying trip in 1795*

Under the sod

Under these trees

Lies the body of Jonathan Pease

He is not here

But only his pod

He has shelled out his peas

And gone to God.

Epitaph in Old North Cemetery, Nantucket,

Massachusetts, transcribed in around 1900

Here lies a man that was Knott born,

His father was Knott before him.

He lived Knott, and did Knott die,

Yet underneath this stone doth lie.

Knott christened,

Knott begot,

And here he lies,

And yet was Knott.

Epitaph from the eighteenth century to a

man named— unsurprisingly—James Knott.

Found in a Sheffield churchyard in England

18 years a maiden

1 year a wife

1 day a mother

Then I lost my life.

> *Epitaph on the tombstone of one Florianna Forbes (d. 1815),*
> *Annapolis Royal, Nova Scotia*

The chief concern of her life for the last twenty-five years was to order and provide for her funeral. Her greatest pleasure was to think and talk about it. She lived many years on a pension of 9d per week, and yet she saved £5, which at her own request was laid out on her funeral.

> *Inscription on the grave of one Mary Broomfield,*
> *who died in 1755 at the grand age of 80, in Cheshire,*
> *England. She was at her big event in body if not in spirit*

Joseph Palmer

Died

Oct. 30, 1873,

84 yrs.

Persecuted for

wearing the beard.

> *Tombstone in Evergreen Cemetery, Leominster, Massachusetts*

Here lies one *More*, and no *More* than he.
One *More*, and no *More*! How can that be?
Why one *More,* and no *More* may well lie here alone:
But here lies one *More*, and that's *More* than one.

Epitaph in St Bennet's Churchyard, Paul's Wharfe,
London, transcribed in 1759

Here lies John's wife, plague of his life;
She spent his wealth, she wronged his health,
And left him daughters three, as bad as she.

Epitaph attributed to "Dr Arbuthnot," 1712.
The grave location is unknown

This spot is the sweetest
I've seen in my life
For it raises my flowers
And covers my wife

Inscription with a double meaning in a churchyard in Wales

Anne Green, a confectioner was by her trade
And also a bit of a sloven,
She was skilled in the art of pies, custard, and tart,
And the consummate skill of the oven.
When she'd lived long enough, she made her last puff,
A puff by her husband much praised,

So here she doth lie, to make her dirt pie,

In the hope that her crust may be raised!

> *Epitaph on a confectioner in Oxford, England*

Alack, and well a day!

Potter himself is turned to clay!

> *Epitaph on a potter*

"Out,"

At 90.

> *Arguably the shortest-ever epitaph, on the grave of a cricketer buried in a Norfolk churchyard*

A Few Ill-Chosen Remarks—Tempting Fate

I'm going to live to be a hundred unless I am run down by a sugar-crazed taxi driver.

> *Jerome Irving Rodale (d. 1971), shortly before his death. The advocate of organic living died of a heart attack aged 72, despite taking extreme care over his food and ingesting over 50 different food supplements each day*

Just keep them for the funeral, although I might give this one a week's extension.

> *Mrs Wilson, who poisoned her new husband; this remark, made about the quantity of baked treats at their wedding reception, gave the game away when it was remembered later by a wedding guest*

Don't come down, Belle, you'll catch your death.

> *Clara Martinelli to her friend Belle Elmore (a.k.a. Cora Crippen) in 1910. Cora's remains were later discovered, and her husband Dr. Crippen was hanged for her murder following a famous manhunt and murder trial*

Just drive down that road, until you get blown up.

> *General George Patton, offering some great advice to*
> *reconnaissance troops. By an ironic twist of fate, old "Blood*
> *and Guts" died in a car accident when his chauffeur-driven*
> *limousine collided with an army truck in Germany in 1945*

I don't mind if my life goes in the service of the nation. If I die today, every drop
of my blood will invigorate the nation.

> *Indira Gandhi (d. 1984), Indian Prime Minister.*
> *She was shot by Sikh militants the next day*

I think I'll go for a drive before dinner. Anyone come along?

> *Donn Byrne (d. 1928), popular author. His car crashed*

Don't you think I'll come back?

> *Rittmeister Manfred Freiherr von Richtofen, "The Red Baron,"*
> *who was Germany's World War I ace pilot, on April 21,*
> *1918—later that day he was shot down in a dogfight*

The only way Terry leaves this band is in a pine box.

> *Manager of the pop group Chicago to assembled members of*
> *the press shortly before the band's lead singer, Kath Terry, shot*
> *himself while joking around playing a pretend game of Russian roulette*
> *in 1978. Terry famously proclaimed, "Don't worry, it's not loaded..."*

I'll need it.

> *Count Bernadotte Folke (d. 1948), United Nations'*
> *mediator, replying to the person who had just wished*
> *him luck. He was assassinated shortly afterward*

At present I am sitting in my cottage and getting used to an empty life.

> *Last diary entry of T.E. Lawrence ("Lawrence of Arabia"), who died the next*
> *day when thrown from his motor-bicycle while swerving to avoid a cyclist*

And I hope your plane crashes!

> *Playful riposte from musician Waylon Jennings to Buddy Holly,*
> *who had jokingly said to his fellow Cricket that he hoped that his bus*
> *would freeze up. Holly died in a plane crash on February 3, 1959—a flight*
> *Jennings would have been on, had he not given up his seat to Big Bopper*

I go to Africa to die there.

> *David Livingstone, before he set out for Africa;*
> *he died there, as he predicted, in 1873*

Do you really think the I. R. A. would think me a worthwhile target?

> *Lord Louis Mountbatten of Burma, British Admiral*
> *and the last Viceroy of India. He was killed in 1979*
> *by a bomb planted on his motor cruiser by the I. R. A.*

What a vigorous old boy that is!

> *An observer, commenting on the hearty demeanor of the*
> *Austrian psychoanalyst Alfred Adler, moments before he*
> *collapsed in Aberdeen, Scotland, and died of heart failure*

If someone is going to kill me, they will kill me.

> *John F. Kennedy (d. 1963), shortly before visiting Dallas*

Well, Mr President, you can't say that the people of Dallas haven't given you a nice welcome.

> *Mrs. John Connally, wife of the then Governor*
> *of Texas, to J.F.K. on his arrival in Dallas*

Being a sex symbol is a heavy load to carry, especially when one is tired, hurt, and bewildered.

> *Marilyn Monroe (Marilyn, the screen goddess,*
> *passes comment on her life shortly before her death)*

I want to avoid all this street violence.

> *One Mrs. McClelland, voicing her reasons for leaving*
> *behind her native Belfast, Northern Ireland, during "*
> *The Troubles," and emigrating to New Zealand. Two years*
> *later, in 1972, she received a fatal blow to the head from a*
> *placard being waved during a civil rights demonstration*

Vancouver, Vancouver, this is it!

> *Last word of David Johnston, who died when*
> *Mount St. Helens erupted on May 18, 1980*

Something dreadful is going to happen to the president today.

> *Jean Dixon, American psychic (correctly) predicting the events of*
> *November 22, 1963, the day JFK was assassinated*

I wish to put him in a position to render a great service to France.

> *"Sweet talk" employed by Charlotte Corday to gain access to*
> *Jean Marat, the revolutionary leader, whom she killed with a kitchen*
> *knife while he lay in his bath (his death is famously depicted in the*
> *painting by Jacques-Louis David). Corday was guillotined for her crime*

Death will come on swift wings to those that disturb the sleep of the Pharaohs.

> *The curse that famously hung over the heads of those involved in*
> *the 1923 expedition to unearth the 3,000-year-old tomb of*
> *Tutankhamun, in Egypt. Two months later, Lord Carnarvon,*
> *leader of the expedition, died mysteriously. His death was*
> *followed by the inexplicable deaths of others that had witnessed*
> *the opening of the tomb of the boy king. "Something dreadful is*
> *going to happen to our family," declared the Hon. Aubrey*
> *Herbert, Carnarvon's half brother. He died on September 27, 1923*

I don't believe in the curse for one moment.

> *Dr. Gamal Mehrez of the Cairo Museum, referring to the "curse" of*
> *Tutankhamun; hours after the boy king's gold mask was dispatched to*
> *London for an exhibition in 1972, the good doctor breathed his last*

Hey, where are the parachutes?

> *Bandleader Glenn Miller was heard to exclaim this on climbing into the*
> *plane in which he later went missing over the English Channel on*
> *December 15, 1944. The reply, from U.S.A.F. pilot Major Norman Baesell*
> *was, "What's the matter, Miller? Do you want to live forever?"*

O fatal urn of my destiny

> *First line of the aria in Verdi's* La Forza del Destino *during*
> *which the American baritone singer Leonard Warren died*
> *of a heart attack at the New York Metropolitan Opera in 1960*

God spoke to me this morning specifically about you, Tom, and He's going to
heal you.

> *Faith healer Robert Tilton, who was sued by Beverly Crowley after*
> *he sent repeated requests to her husband for donations, promising*
> *to heal him (her husband, Tom, had been dead for five months)*

Fijians are not lovers of human flesh.

Thus claimed the Reverend Thomas Baker, a British missionary
who was hacked to death with a battleaxe by said Fijians,
then served up with a traditional vegetable relish. Baker was the
only white victim of cannibalism in Fiji—dubbed "the Cannibal
Isles" by contemporary explorers—during the tumultuous colonial
era. The reverend had been duped. "We ate everything but his
boots," said a Fijian native who had partaken of him in 1867

I have seen so many eruptions in the last 20 years that I don't care if I die
tomorrow.

Maurice Krafft, volcanologist, speaking the day before he was
killed on Mount Unzen, a volcano in Japan, in 1991

Why not send out this new call, S.O.S.—it might be your last chance.

A Marconi operator, joking on hearing that the "unsinkable"
Titanic had sent out an emergency alert, on April 15, 1912

No matter what else, he is not a killer.

Loyal mom Bessie Gilmore, before her son Gary was executed
on two counts of murder in the state of Utah

The wind is stronger in the street than up here!

> *At the age of 73, legendary tightrope walker Karl Wallenda tempted fate in San Juan, Puerto Rico in 1978. He was attempting to walk across a wire stretched between two hotels and fell to his death, blown off balance by the high winds*

Not being able to banish the figure [of Mr. Bannister dressed as Polly Peachum] from her memory, she was thrown into hysterics, which continued without intermission until she expired Friday morning.

> *The* Gentleman's Magazine *of April 1782 reporting the death of Mrs. Fitzherbert, who had been to see* The Beggar's Opera *at the famous Drury Lane Theatre in London. The performance had provoked gales of laughter among the audience, but none laughed so much as Mrs. Fitzherbert. In fact, she could be said to have had the last laugh*

See how long it takes me to eat this.

> *One Alan McLaren, about to stuff his mouth with chocolate. Mr. McLaren later died of asphyxiation*

Look, here's one you haven't seen before.

> *Anthony J. Drexel III (d. 1893), American socialite, showing guests the latest artifact to be added to his family's personal arsenal on display in their gun room and accidentally shooting himself fatally in the process*

Now son, pull.

> *One Vincent Benny, showing his two-year-old son*
> *how to use a revolver—the toddler, unfortunately for*
> *his father, proved to be a fast learner and quick on the draw*

There's nothing about my life that is an accident

> *Marc Bolan of the Seventies glam rock band T-Rex, shortly before*
> *his fatal car crash. A mini driven by girlfriend Gloria Jones veered*
> *off the road next to Barnes Common in London and hit a tree, killing*
> *Bolan instantly. Today, the tree the car struck is still decorated by fans*

Valavoir.

> *Last utterance of Count Valavoir, French general serving under the*
> *seventeenth-century soldier Viscount Turenne, answering a sentry's*
> *challenge one evening as he returned after curfew. The sentry took offence*
> *at being told "va le voir" ("go and see") and shot poor Valavoir dead*

Let's see if this will do it.

> *Jon Erik Hexum, actor (d. 1984), who shot himself by*
> *accident (he had a blank-loaded pistol) while on the set of*
> *the TV spy show* Cover Up; *he died six days later*

Hey guys, watch this!

> *Todd Poller, who choked on a live fish in 2001*

I did not think they would put a young gentleman to death for such a trifle.

Jean-François le Fevre Barre (d. 1766),
condemned to death for having defaced a crucifix

I don't need bodyguards.

Comment by union leader Jimmy Hoffa in a
Playboy *interview, December 1975—he subsequently*
went missing and was never seen again

So Long, Farewell, Auf Wiedersehen, Adieu— Farewell Speeches

I have found it impossible to carry the heavy burden of responsibility and to discharge my duties as King as I would wish to do without the help and support of the woman I love.

> *Extract from the abdication speech of Edward VIII, 1936, who couldn't carry on without Wallis Simpson at his side*

If I should die, think only this of me:
That there is some corner of a foreign field
That is for ever England.

> *Rupert Brooke, World War I poet—prophetic words, for he died in 1915 crossing the Aegean sea en route to the battle at Gallipoli*

Good-bye dearie, I'll see you later.

> *Colonel John Jacob Astor IV, who went down with the* Titanic *in 1912, bidding farewell to his wife, who was already in a lifeboat and chivalrously refusing to take up any space himself*

Please know that I am quite aware of the hazards. I want to do it because I
want to do it. Women must try to do things as men have tried. When they fail,
their failure must be but a challenge to others.

*Amelia Earhart (d. 1937), aviation pioneer, in what was to be a final letter to
her husband before she attempted her ill-fated flight across the Pacific*

When everybody down to the groundskeepers and those boys in white coats
remember you with trophies—that's something. When you have a wonderful
mother-in-law who takes sides with you in squabbles with her own
daughter—that's something. When you have a father and a mother who work
all their lives so you can have an education and build your body—it's a
blessing. When you have a wife who has been a tower of strength and shown
more courage than you dreamed existed—the finest I know. So I close in
saying that I may have had a tough break, but I have an awful lot to live for.
Thank you.

*Part of the speech delivered at the Yankee Stadium in 1939 by
Lou Gehrig, when the baseball hero knew he was dying.
Understandably, there wasn't a dry eye in the house*

I herewith renounce for all time claims to the throne of Prussia and to the
German Imperial throne connected herewith.

*Abdication of Wilhelm II, Kaiser of Germany,
in the closing months of World War I, 1918*

I lay not my blood on you, or on my people, and demand no other compensation
for any punishment than the return of peace and a revival of the fidelity which
the kingdom owes to my children.

I die a Christian, according to the profession of the Church of England, as I
found it left me by my father. I needed not to have come here; and therefore I
tell you, and I pray to God it may not be laid to your charge, that I am the
Martyr of the People.

> *Charles I (d. 1649), King of England, on the*
> *scaffold where he was to be beheaded*

Now I stretch out my hand, and from the further shore I bid adieu to all who
have cared to read any among the many words I have written.

> *Anthony Trollope (d. 1882), British novelist—*
> *the final lines of his autobiography*

Why should I fear death? I have seen him often. When he comes he'll seem like
an old friend. If I were to die, my last words would be "Have faith and pursue
the unknown end."

> *Oliver Wendell Holmes (d. 1935), jurist. His last words,*
> *when the time actually came, were "damn foolery!"*

I am signing my death warrant.

> *Michael Collins (d. 1921), Irish patriot killed shortly after*
> *signing the Irish Treaty of 1921, to which he is referring*

Lunch—Tuesday—wet—fine—cottage one mile Bovington Camp—Shaw

> *Last telegram sent by "Aircraftsman Shaw," the identity latterly*
> *assumed by T.E. Lawrence, author of* The Seven Pillars of Wisdom
> *and better known as "Lawrence of Arabia" for his role in the fight*
> *for Arab independence against the Turks. Lawrence was killed in a*
> *motorbike accident on a country lane close to his cottage in Dorset in 1935*

I hope to be in Phil. in about ten days. I am stronger than for years, but take no
new responsibilities.

> *Final telegram sent by Catherine Beecher (d. 1878),*
> *American feminist pioneer*

I have no plans. I am in search of that most elusive of all forms of
happiness—rest.

> *Former British Prime Minister Ramsay MacDonald,*
> *as he was about to embark on a "restful" cruise on*
> *November 4, 1937. He died while at sea five days later*

I paraphrase Castro on trial after Moncada: I warn you, gentlemen, I have only
just begun!

> *George Jackson (d. 1971), black rights activist. This was in his last letter to a*
> *book publisher, two months before being gunned down*

Camp will be bulging by the time I leave for America in March, but right now it is awfully quiet.

> *Closing line of last—unfinished—letter written*
> *by Dian Fossey (d. 1985), of* Gorillas in the Mist *fame.*
> *She was murdered in her hut in Rwanda*

Agnes, darling, if such should be we never meet again, while firing my last shot I will gently breathe the name of my wife—Agnes—and with wishes even for my enemies, I will make the plunge and try to swim to the other shore.

> *"Wild Bill" Hickok (d. 1876), hero of the American West*

I hope we shall be done justice to. We have fulfilled our task but we have been abandoned. We have not been followed up as we expected. And the depot party abandoned their post. King behaved nobly. He stayed with me to the last and placed the pistol in my hand, leaving me lying on the surface as I wished.

> *Robert O'Hara Burke (d. 1861), explorer, who died of starvation while*
> *attempting to cross the continent of Australia—this was his last note*

God knows I am sorry to be the cause of sorrow to anyone in the world, but everyone must die and at every death there must be some sorrow. All the things I had hoped to do with you after this Expedition are as nothing now, but there are greater things for us to do in the world to come. My only regret is leaving you to struggle through your life alone, but I may be coming to you by a quicker way. I feel so happy now in having got time to write to you. One of my notes will surely reach you. Dad's little compass and Mother's little

comb are in my pocket. Your little testament and prayer book will be in my
hand or in my breast pocket when the end comes. All is well.

*Edward Wilson (d. 1912), explorer and doctor on the
ill-fated Antarctic expedition led by Captain Scott (this was
Wilson's last letter, which he addressed to his wife)*

For God's sake, look after our people.

*Robert Falcon Scott, Captain Scott, of the Antarctic (d. 1912). It
was the final entry in his Journal, dated March 29, 1912, on the
famously doomed expedition to the South Pole, where the party
found they had been beaten by the Norwegian, Amundsen*

Have struck iceberg. Badly damaged. Rush aid.

Last S.O.S. message from the Titanic, *which sank in 1912*

Seeing how much I have been favored in my present progress, I am full of hope
that our Almighty Protector will allow me to bring my darling scheme to a
successful termination.

*Dr. Ludwig Leichhardt (d. 1848) in his last letter;
he was later lost in the jungle and never traced*

I shall only add, respecting myself, that, having experienced the goodness of
that Being in conducting me prosperously through a long life, I have no doubt
of its continuance in the next, though without the smallest conceit of
meriting such goodness.

Extract from one of the last letters written by Benjamin Franklin (d. 1790)

I know the color...That drop of blood is my death warrant.

> *John Keats, English Romantic poet, on discovering in February*
> *1820 that he was coughing blood. He died twelve months later*

I'm not at all afraid of the thought of death and look forward to it. It would be
lovely if there were a song or two... and someone said some nice happy words
about me...

> *Letter written by Muppets creator Jim Henson (d. 1990)*
> *four years before he died of a heart attack with*
> *instructions for it to be opened only after his death*

This is my final word. It is time for me to become an apprentice once more.
I have not settled in which direction. But somewhere, sometime, soon.

> *Final public statement of Lord Beaverbrook (d. 1964), newspaper magnate*

Tomorrow I shall have finished this (the *Scented Garden*) and I promise you that
I will never write another book on this subject. I will take to our biography.

> *Sir Richard Burton's (d. 1890) last words to his wife.*
> *He was translator of the* Kama Sutra

My dear friends (Anderson and Scott) are both dead; but though all Europeans
who are with me should die, and though I were myself half dead, I would still
persevere; and if I could not succeed in the object of my journey, I would at
least die on the Niger.

> *Mungo Park (d. 1806), the Victorian explorer who journeyed to*
> *the heart of Africa, in his last letter to Lord Camden*

Like anybody else, I would like to live a long life. But I'm not concerned with that. I see the Promised Land. I may not get there with you, but mine eyes have seen the glory...

Martin Luther King, speaking at the Mason Street Temple the evening before he was assassinated by James Earl Ray in Memphis, Tennessee. Those closest to him felt the civil rights leader was unduly preoccupied with thoughts of death

Southerly gales, squalls, lee rail under water, wet bunks, hard tack, bully beef— wish you were here, instead of me!

Last message from Richard Halliburton, American adventurer, who died in 1939 while attempting to sail a Chinese junk from Hong Kong to San Francisco

I leave California Wednesday following. Daddy.

Last telegram received from the American author Jack London (d. 1916)

I have come to say goodbye... in a quarter of an hour I will be dead... They suspect me of having taken part in the plot to kill Hitler. It seems my name was on Goerdeler's list to be President of the Reich... I have never seen Goerdeler in my life... The Führer has given me the choice of taking poison or being hauled before the People's Court. They have brought the poison.

Erwin Rommel (d. 1944), German Field Marshall nicknamed the "Desert Fox" during World War II and greatly respected by Allied commanders. His farewell was to his wife. He took the poison: "I will never allow myself to be hanged by that man Hitler"

I've had a very happy childhood. I've had a good time as a young man. And I've had a terrific middle age. The only thing that I'm disappointed in is that I was looking forward to having a good old age, too.

> *Oscar Hammerstein II (d. 1960), American lyricist. (He was speaking on his 65th birthday, when he knew he was dying of cancer)*

I inhabit a weak, frail, decayed tenement, battered by the winds and broken in on by the storms. And, from all I can learn, the landlord does not intend to repair.

> *John Quincy Adams (d. 1848), sixth president of the United States, during his final illness*

I do not want a lying official epitaph. Write on my tomb that I was the faithful servant of my master, the Emperor Wilhelm [I], King of Prussia.

> *Count Otto Von Bismarck (d. 1898), German statesman nicknamed "The Iron Chancellor." He fell out with Wilhelm II and quit his post*

Dear Joe Moscrop... Still some strength in me. I write a line to shake you by the hand; our friendship has been entirely pleasant. I am very ill with bronchitis. With best wishes for the New Year.

> *Thought to be the last letter written by Beatrix Potter (d. 1943), English writer of such children's classics as* Peter Rabbit. *She died just before Christmas from the nagging cold to which she refers in her letter, which was probably written to an animal-loving friend*

I don't know what I may seem to the world. But as to myself, I seem to have
  been only a boy playing on the seashore and diverting myself in now and
  then finding a smoother pebble or prettier shell than the ordinary, whilst the
  great ocean of truth lay all undiscovered before me.

> *Sir Isaac Newton (d. 1727), English scientist,*
> *who formulated the theory of gravity*

Mom, do you hear the rain? Do you hear the rain? Mom, I just want to take off in
  the plane.

> *The remark of the seven-year-old pilot prodigy Jessica Dubroff (d. 1996),*
> *in a phone call to her mother, as she embarked on her attempt to*
> *become the youngest person to fly across the U.S.—minutes later,*
> *she crashed her plane, killing herself, her father, and another*

"Exit Stage Left—
Famous Last Movie Lines "

Top of the world, Ma!

> *Cody Jarrett (James Cagney) in* White Heat *(1949)—the psychotic gangster yells to his mother before blowing himself up in the oil refinery*

You know the penalty for failure.

> *Ming the Merciless—the last words heard by the many who would disappoint Ming, Emperor of the Planet Mongo, arch enemy of Flash Gordon (1980)*

A toast before we go into battle!

> *Last line spoken by Gareth (Simon Callow) before he collapses and dies of a heart attack in* Four Weddings and A Funeral *(1994)*

I am at peace with God. My quarrel is with Man.

> *Charlie Chaplin as Monsieur Henri Verdoux, in the movie of the same name (1947), to the priest who wants to give him last rites before he is led off to the guillotine*

The horror! The horror!

> *The last words of Kurtz in* The Heart of Darkness, *a novel*
> *by Joseph Conrad and of the Marlon Brando character in the*
> *Francis Ford Coppola movie* Apocalypse Now *(1979)*

Mother of mercy! Is this the end of Rico?

> *Edward G. Robinson who is Rico, a gangster (modeled on Al Capone)—the*
> *last words of the character and of the movie—in* Little Caesar *(1930)*

Mr. Corleone is man who insists on hearing good news fast.

> *Tom Hagen (Robert Duvall) in* The Godfather *(1972), when*
> *Don Corleone hears the news, the prize stallion dies*

Just head for the big star straight on. [Pointing to the heavens] The highways
  under it take us right home.

> *Clark Gable to Marilyn Monroe in* The Misfits *(1961), answering her*
> *question "How do you find your way back in the dark?" (Ironically, Gable*
> *died of a heart attack just a few days after shooting on the film had finished)*

Take me! Take me!

> *Father Damien Carrass (Jason Miller) at the end of* The Exorcist
> *(1973), offers himself to the demon to save Linda Blair*

Daisy, Daisy, give me your answer do. I'm half-crazy, all for the love of you.

> *HAL 9000 (The computer in* 2001: A Space Odyssey *(1968)*
> *sings as he is shut down by Lt. Bowman)*

I've got the gun!

> *Jim Stark (James Dean), in* Rebel Without A Cause *(1955), screams at the cops who are about to gun down his friend Plato, played by Sal Mineo*

Tara! Home! I'll go home, and I'll think of some way to get him back. After all, tomorrow is another day!

> *Final lines spoken by Scarlett O'Hara (Vivien Leigh) in* Gone with the Wind *(1939) from the book of the same name by Margaret Mitchell*

I've seen things you people wouldn't believe. Attack ships on fire off the shoulder of Orion. I watched c-beams ... glitter in the dark near Tanhauser Gate. All those ... moments will be lost ... in time, like tears ... in rain. Time ...to die.

> *Last words of Roy Batty, the replicant in* Blade Runner *(1982) directed by Ridley Scott, screenplay by David Webb Peoples*

On no. It wasn't the airplanes. It was beauty killed the beast.

> *The character Carl Denham (Robert Armstrong) speaking the last line in* King Kong *(1933) in response to the police officer, who had said: "Well, Denham, the airplanes got him." The line harks back to the opening scenes of the film, which showed an old Arabian proverb: "And lo, the beast looked upon the face of beauty. And it stayed its hand from killing. And from that day, it was dead"*

All right, Mr. De Mille, I'm ready for my close up.

Gloria Swanson, Norma in Sunset Boulevard *(1950),*
in the closing line of the movie

Well, nobody's perfect.

Famous closing line of the movie Some Like it Hot *(1959), starring*
Marilyn Monroe, Jack Lemmon. It's delivered by Osgood, trying to persuade
Daphne (Lemmon as "Jerry") to marry him, in response to Daphne-Jerry's
confession: "We can't get married at all... I'm a man"

Shut up and deal!

Shirley MacLaine, as Fran, in the Billy Wilder movie The Apartment *(1960)*
to C. C. "Bud" Baxter (Jack Lemmon), who had declared, hopelessly,
"Did you hear what I said, Miss Kubelik? I absolutely adore you"

I hope they are watching. They'll see—they'll see—and they'll know and they'll
say, why she wouldn't even harm a fly.

Anthony Perkins, speaking as "mother," in Psycho *(1960)*

Lady, I don't have the time.

A dying Lee Marvin, after shooting Ronald Reagan in the film The Killers
(1964), responding to Angie Dickinson's pleas for mercy

There have been tyrants and murderers and for a time they can seem invincible,
but in the end they always fall. Think of it. Always.

Words spoken—posthumously, as a voiceover—by Gandhi
(Ben Kingsley) in the 1982 movie of the same name

Brody: I used to hate the water.

Hooper: I can't imagine why.

> *Last lines of the movie* Jaws *(1975), exchanged between Brody (Roy
> Schneider) and Hooper (Richard Dreyfuss) as they paddle toward the shore*

What do I do now?

> *Closing line of* The Candidate *(1972), when McKay
> (Robert Redford) has finally made it to the White House*

Never you mind, honey, never you mind.

> *Closing line of the movie* The Last Picture Show *(1971), starring Jeff Bridges
> and Cybill Shepherd. It is delivered, in a spirit of generosity, by Ruth*

Mein Führer, I can walk!

> *Dr. Strangelove (Peter Sellers), miraculously mobile, having detonated the
> Doomsday Machine to destroy the world in the movie* Dr. Strangelove, Or:
> How I Learned To Stop Worrying and Love The Bomb *(1964)*

Where are your troubles now? Forgotten, I told you so. We have no troubles
here. Here, life is beautiful. The girls are beautiful. Even the orchestra is
beautiful.

> *Closing line of the movie* Cabaret *(1972)*

It ain't like it used to be, but, uh, it'll do.

> *Sykes (Edmund O'Brien) to fellow outlaws, shown setting off to join the
> Mexican Revolution in* The Wild Bunch *(1969), as the final credits roll*

If any of my circuits or gears would help, I'd gladly donate them.

C-3PO to R2-D2 in the closing sequence of the 1977 movie
Star Wars (Episode IV: A New Hope)

Toto, we're home! Home! ...And I'm not gonna leave here ever, ever again, because I love you all! And oh, Auntie Em, there's no place like home.

Dorothy (16-year-old Judy Garland), safely back in Kansas with her dog Toto, in the movie The Wizard of Oz *(1939)*

I'm an average nobody. I get to live the rest of my life as a schnook.

Henry Hill (Ray Liotta), at the end of the Martin Scorsese movie GoodFellas *(1990)*

Rich fellas come up and they die and their kids ain't no good and they die out. But we keep a-comin'. We're the people that live. They can't wipe us out. They can't lick us. We'll go on forever, Pa... 'cause... we're the people.

Closing line of the movie The Grapes of Wrath *(1940), based on the novel of the same name by John Steinbeck*

Where are you guys going? Wait a minute! I'll remember this! I'll remember everyone of ya! I'll be back—don't you forget that. I'll be back.

Johnny Friday (Lee. J. Cobb) in the movie On the Waterfront *(1954), starring Marlon Brando*

I'll be waiting for you. If they hang you, I'll always remember you.

> *Sam Spade (Humphrey Bogart) handing over Brigid O'Shaughnessy*
> *(Mary Astor) to the police in the movie* The Maltese Falcon *(1941)*
> *based on the 1929 novel by Dashiell Hammett*

I'll be right here.

> *E.T. bidding farewell to Elliot and touching the boy's forehead*
> *in the Spielberg movie,* E.T., The Extraterrestrial *(1982)*

I do wish we could chat longer, but I'm having an old friend for dinner. Bye.

> *Hannibal Lecter (Anthony Hopkins) to Clarice in*
> *the movie* The Silence of the Lambs *(1991), based on the*
> *1988 Thomas Harris novel of the same name*

My god, it's full of stars.

> *Dave Bowman—the last words in* 2001: A Space Odyssey*(1968)*

If history had taught us anything it's that you can kill anyone.

> *Michael Corleone's (Al Pacino's) observation before unleashing*
> *the final massacre of his enemies in* The Godfather: Part II (*1974*)

Hang on a minute, lads, I've got a great idea... er... er.

> *Charlie (Michael Caine), and the last line in the movie that made mini*
> *motorcars super-famous,* The Italian Job *(1969)—the lads' vehicle is*
> *balanced on the edge of a cliff, with only the gold bullion balancing it*

I'm going to have to open it.

> *Detective Somerset played by Morgan Freeman decides to open*
> *the grisly package sent by serial killer John Doe at the end*
> *of* Se7en *(1995), directed by David Fincher*

Haven't got a sensible name, Calloway.

> *Closing line of the movie* The Third Man *(1949), spoken by*
> *Joseph Cotton as the suitably inappropriately named Holly Martins*

The greatest trick the Devil ever pulled was to convince the world he didn't exist.

> *Verbal Kint, before he vanishes, in* The Usual Suspects *(1995)*

Give me a girl at an impressionable age, and she is mine for life.

> *Closing line of* The Prime of Miss Jean Brodie *(1969),*
> *delivered by Maggie Smith as Jean Brodie*

Cricket: Hey, Slim. Are you still happy?
Slim: What do think?

> *Closing lines of the movie* To Have and Have Not *(1944),*
> *between Hoagy Carmichael and Lauren Bacall (Slim)*

Go get 'em, champ... I'm the boss, I'm the boss, I'm the boss, I'm the boss... boss, boss, boss, boss, boss, boss.

> *Closing line of the movie* Raging Bull *(1980), delivered by*
> *Robert de Niro (to himself in the mirror) as boxer Jake LaMotta*

I was wrong about you... I thought Christmas only comes once a year.

Pierce Brosnan as 007, in bed with Dr Christmas Jones, in the Bond movie
The World is not Enough *(1999)—closing line of the film*

Hello everybody. This is Mrs. Norman Maine.

Closing line of the 1954 movie A Star is Born *, starring Judy Garland—a remake of the 1937 film, keeping the same last line*

To die, to be really dead, that might be glorious.

The indefatigable and ever-thirsty Count Dracula ("I never drink...wine"), in the 1931 movie Dracula, *with Bela Lugosi in the title role*

The world shall hear from me again!

Closing line of the movie The Face of Fu Manchu *(1965). Boris Karloff says the same thing at the end of* The Mask of Fu Manchu *(1931)*

Feed me, Seymour!

The hungry carnivorous plant, which invariably gets what it wants, in The Little Shop of Horrors *(1960)*

The old man was right, only the farmers won. We lost. We always lose.

Yul Brynner; closing line of the movie
The Magnificent Seven *(1960)*

Eliza, where the devil are my slippers?

Closing line of the movie My Fair Lady *(1964), delivered*
by Rex Harrison as Professor Henry Higgins

Yowsir, Yowsir, Yowsir! Here they are again—these wonderful, wonderful kids,
still struggling, still hoping as the clock of fate ticks away. The dance of
destiny continues. The marathon goes on and on and on. How long can they
last? Let's here it. C'mon, let's hear it. Let's hear it.

Closing lines of the movie They Shoot Horses Don't They *(1969),*
whipping up enthusiasm for another dance marathon

Welcome to Hollywood! What's your dream? Everybody comes here. This is
Hollywood, land of dreams. Some dreams come true, some don't, but keep on
dreamin'. This is Hollywood. Always time to dream. So keep on dreamin'.

Closing line—a happy passer-by's voiceover—
in the movie Pretty Woman *(1990)*

Take off the red shoes.

Closing line of the movie The Red Shoes *(1948),*
as Moira Page is dying

Marry me and I'll never look at any other horse.

Closing line of the Groucho Marx movie A Day at the Races *(1937)*

My dear, there's a little bit of Don Juan in every man, but since I am Don Juan, there must be more of it in me.

> *Closing line of* The Adventures of Don Juan *(1949)*
> *delivered by swashbuckler Errol Flynn (as Don Juan)*

And I felt His voice take the sword out of my hand.

> *Closing line of* Ben Hur *(1959) delivered by*
> *Charlton Heston, as the eponymous freed slave*

Even if we, the gods, are abandoned or forgotten, the stars will never fade, never. They will burn till the end of time.

> *Closing line of the movie* Clash of the Titans *(1981),*
> *delivered by Laurence Olivier (Zeus)*

Madness! Madness!

> *Closing line of the classic prisoner-of-war movie* The Bridge on the
> River Kwai *(1957), as Clipton (James Donald) surveys the wreckage—*
> *material and human—around the now-destroyed bridge of the title*

It's hard to stay mad when there's so much beauty in the world... I can't feel anything but gratitude for every single moment of my stupid little life.

> *Kevin Spacey, as the character Lester Burnham, talks*
> *from beyond the grave in* American Beauty *(1999)*

I'm the tyranny of evil men. But I'm tryin' real hard to be the shepherd.

> *Samuel L. Jackson sees the light at the end of* Pulp Fiction *(1994)*

This is Ripley, W564502460H, executive officer, last survivor of the commercial
starship Nostromo signing off.

> *Sigourney Weaver breathing a sigh of relief at the end of* Alien *(1979)*

I have always depended on the kindness of strangers.

> *Vivien Leigh as Blanche Dubois in the film* A Streetcar Named Desire *(1951)*
> *by Tennessee Williams, as she is taken away to a mental institution*

I know why you came, and it's awfully good of you. There's some magazines
here. If you'll stop to lunch I'll prove you this time traveling up to the hilt,
specimen and all. If you'll forgive my leaving you now?

> *The narrator bids farewell in* The Time Machine
> *by H.G. Wells to travel to the time of the Warlocks*

It is a far, far better thing I do now than I have ever done, it is far, far better rest I
go to than I have ever known.

> *Sidney Carlton in Charles Dickens'* Tale of Two Cities
> *(1958), as he goes to the guillotine in the place of a better man*

Never let go.

> *Jack (Leonardo DiCaprio) to Rose (Kate Winslet) in the last scene*
> *of* Titanic, *written and directed by James Cameron*

Louis, I think this is the beginning of a beautiful friendship.

> *The last words Rick (Humphrey Bogart) speaks*
> *in the final scene of* Casablanca *(1942) when Rick has*
> *said fairwell to (Ilsa) Ingrid Bergman at the airport*

Hit it.

> *Last words said by Thelma (Geena Davis) to Louise*
> *(Susan Sarandon) just before they drive over the edge of a*
> *cliff at the end of the film* Thelma and Louise *(1991). Moments*
> *before Thelma says: "You're a good friend," to which*
> *Louise replies, "You, too, sweetie, the best." Then the B. B. King*
> *song "Better Not Look Down" begins and Louise asks,*
> *"Are you sure?" and Thelma nods replying "Hit it"*

Way to go, Paula! Way to go!

> *A fellow office worker applauds as Debra Winger's*
> *character is carried off by a uniformed Richard Gere at the*
> *end of* An Officer and A Gentleman *(1982)*

Get him away from her! He's responsible for everything!

> *Jack Nicholson discovers the unpleasant truth in the*
> *finale of Roman Polanski's* Chinatown *(1974)*

In case I don't see you—good afternoon, good evening, and good night.

> *Truman signs off from* The Truman Show *(1998)*

But what we found out is that each one of us is a brain...and an athlete...and a basket case...and a princess...and a criminal...Does that answer your question? Sincerely yours, the Breakfast Club.

> *Teenage angst and realizations at the end of John Hughes'*
> *bratpack film* The Breakfast Club *(1985)*

Where we are going, we don't use roads.

> *Dr. Emmet Brown to Marty McFly in the*
> *1985 film* Back to the Future

Oh Captain, my Captain.

> *The pupils pay tribute to Mr. Keating, played by Robin Williams,*
> *in the final scene of* Dead Poets Society *(1989)*

The End—
Famous Last Book Lines

Even now I can't altogether believe that any of this has really happened...

Closing line of the book Goodbye to Berlin *by*
Christopher Isherwood

So I awoke, and behold it was a dream.

Closing line of The Pilgrim's Progress *by John Bunyan*

"It is Clarissa," he said. For there she was.

Last line of the novel Mrs Dalloway *by Virginia Woolf*

The tomb bore the names of Tom and Maggie Tulliver, and below the names it
was written—
"In their death they were not divided."

Closing lines of the novel The Mill on the Floss *by George Eliot*
(pseudonym of Mary Ann, or Marian, Evans)

Don't tell anybody anything. If you do, you start missing everybody.

Last line of Catcher in the Rye, *by J.D. Salinger*

Here is what Kilgore Trout cried out to me in my father's voice: "Make me young, make me young!"

Last line of Breakfast of Champions *by Kurt Vonnegut Jr.*

It was done; it was finished. Yes, she thought, laying down her brush in extreme fatigue, I have had my vision.

Closing line of To the Lighthouse *by Virginia Woolf*

Three dangerous men gone for parts unknown.

Last line from The Big Nowhere, *by James Ellroy*

But to us it seems that this will be a good place to stop.

Last line of Notes from the Underground, *by Fyodor Dostoyevsky*

She walked rapidly in the thin June sunlight towards the worst horror of all.

Last line of Brighton Rock *by Graham Greene*

Poor Crabbin...poor all of us when you come to think of it.

Last line of The Third Man, *by Graham Greene*

For some reason this made him laugh and he began to imitate the siren as loud as he could.

Last line of The Day of the Locust *by Nathaniel West*

Vladimir: Well, shall we go?

Estragon: Yes, let's go.

(They do not move.)

> *Last line of the play* Waiting for Godot*, by Samuel Becket*

I fell in love in James Tyrone and was so happy for a time.

> *Last line of* Long Day's Journey into Night *by Eugene O'Neill*

Father McConnell says prayers help. If you've got this far, send up one for me,
    and Cora, and make it that we're together, wherever it is.

> *Last line of* The Postman Always Rings Twice *by James M. Cain*

As he fell, Leamas saw a small car smashed between great lorries, and the
    children waving cheerfully through the window.

> *Last line of* The Spy Who Came in from the Cold *by John LeCarré*

The old man was dreaming about the lions.

> *Last line of* The Old Man and The Sea *by Ernest Hemingway*

It was by means of them that he hoped one day to restore Hetton to the glory
    that it had enjoyed in the days of his cousin Tony.

> *Last line of* A Handful of Dust *by Evelyn Waugh*

But, if the spirits of the Dead ever come back to earth, to visit spots hallowed by
    the love—the love beyond the grave—of those whom they knew in life, I
    believe that the shade of Agnes sometimes hovers round that solemn nook.

I believe it none the less, because that nook is in a Church, and she was weak and erring.

Last line of Oliver Twist *by Charles Dickens*

He has just been awarded the Legion of Honor.

Last line of Madame Bovary *by Gustave Flaubert,*
referring to the pompous chemist, Homais

He heard it and sank deeper than sorrow, through torn sobs and cries toward the consummation of his heart's ultimate need.

Last line of Seize the Day *by Saul Bellow*

And Carlson said, "Now what the hell ya suppose is eatin' them two guys?"

Last line of Of Mice and Men *by John Steinbeck*

It was calling to itself every boat on the river, every one, the whole town, and the sky, and the country and us, all of it being called away, and the Seine too, everything—let's hear no more of all this.

Closing sentence of Journey to the End of the Night (Voyage au
bout de la nuit), *the novel by Louis-Ferdinand Céline*

Somebody threw a dead dog after him down the ravine.

Closing sentence of Under the Volcano *by Malcolm Lowry*

I felt like a monster reincarnation of Horatio Alger...a Man on the Move, and just
   sick enough to be totally confident.

> *Last line of* Fear and Loathing in Las Vegas
> *by Hunter S. Thompson*

So we beat on, boats against the current, borne back ceaselessly into the past.

> *Closing line of* The Great Gatsby *by F. Scott Fitzgerald*

And wise Uncle Venner, passing slowly from the ruinous porch, seemed to hear
   a strain of music, and fancied that sweet Alice Pyncheon—after witnessing
   these deeds, this bygone woe and this present happiness, of her kindred
   mortals—had given one farewell touch of a spirit's joy upon her harpsichord,
   as she floated heavenward from the HOUSE OF THE SEVEN GABLES!

> *Closing words of* The House of the Seven Gables
> *by Nathaniel Hawthorne*

Silent, upon a peak in Darien.

> *Last line of* On First Looking Into Chapman's Homer
> *a poem by John Keats*

But he is not always alone. When the long winter nights come on and the
   wolves follow their meat into the lower valleys, he may be seen running at the
   head of the pack through the pale moonlight or glimmering borealis, leaping
   gigantic above his fellows, his great throat a-bellow as he sings a song of the
   younger world, which is the song of the pack.

> *Closing words of* The Call of The Wild *by Jack London*

He remembered the days when you could get thirteen Royal Natives for a
shilling.

Last line of The Moon and Sixpence *by W. Somerset Maugham*

He smiled and took her hand and pressed it. The got up and walked out of the
gallery. They stood for a moment at the balustrade and looked at Trafalgar
Square. Cabs and omnibuses hurried to and fro, and crowds passed,
hastening in every direction, and the sun was shining.

Last line of Of Human Bondage *by W. Somerset Maugham*

Buoyed up by that coffin, for almost one whole day and night, I floated on a soft
and dirge-like main. The unharming sharks, they glided by as if with padlocks
on their mouths; the savage sea-hawks sailed with sheathed beaks. On the
second day, a sail drew near, nearer, and picked me up at last. It was the
devious-cruising Rachel, that in her retracing search after her missing
children, only found another orphan.

Closing lines of Moby Dick *by Herman Melville*

They hand in hand, with wandering steps and slow,
Through Eden took their solitary way.

Last verses of the epic poem Paradise Lost *by John Milton*

It was chiefly in order to allow time for the preliminary work of translation that
the final adoption of Newspeak had been fixed for so late a date as 2050.

Closing line of 1984, *written in 1949 by George Orwell*

The creatures outside looked from pig to man, and from man to pig, and from
pig to man again; but already it was impossible to say which was which.

Closing line of Animal Farm *by George Orwell*

Only that day dawns to which we are awake. There is more day to dawn. The
sun is but a morning star.

Closing words of Walden *by Henry David Thoreau*

Tom's most well now, and got his bullet around his neck on a watch guard for a
watch, and is always seeing what time it is, and so there ain't nothing more to
write about, and I am rotten glad of it, because if I'd 'a' knowed what a
trouble it was to make a book I wouldn't 'a' tackled it, and ain't a-going to no
more. But I reckon I got to light out for the territory ahead of the rest, because
Aunt Sally she's going to adopt me and sivilize me, and I can't stand it. I been
there before.

Closing lines of Huckleberry Finn *by Mark Twain*

John Thomas says good-night to Lady Jane, a little droopingly, but with a
hopeful heart.

Closing lines of Lady Chatterley's Lover *by D.H. Lawrence*

Sometimes she missed the Bear Creek days, when she and he had ridden
together, and sometimes she declared that his work would kill him. But it
does not seem to have done so. Their eldest boy rides the horse Monte; and,
strictly between ourselves, I think his father is going to live a long while.

Closing words of The Virginian—Horseman of the Plain *by Owen Wister*

I took her hand in mine, and we went out of the ruined place; and, as the morning mists had risen long ago when I first left the forge, so, the evening mists were rising now, and in all the broad expanse of tranquil light they showed to me, I saw no shadow of another parting from her.

Closing lines of Great Expectations *by Charles Dickens*

O God, You've done enough, You've robbed me of enough, I'm too tired and old to learn to love, leave me alone for ever.

Closing line of The End of the Affair *by Graham Greene*

My day has been too long. In the morning I saw the sons of Unamis happy and strong; and yet, before the night has come, have I lived to see the last warrior of the wise race of the Mohicans.

Closing line of The Last of the Mohicans
by James Fennimore Cooper

Sometimes being a bitch is all a woman has to hold on to.

Dolores Claiborne (Stephen King's heroine in the novel of the same name reacts ruefully to being the prime suspect in two deaths)

"Wrong, Wrong, Wrong—
No Foresight Required

"

I'd rather be dead than singing Satisfaction when I'm 45.

Mick Jagger, still touring with the Stones at 60

I don't want to be up on a stage singing Twist and Shout when I'm 30.

John Lennon

The US will have its first woman president elected in 1980.

Jean Dixon, famous American psychic—
more often famously wrong than famously right

This is a dull war. There is no shooting.

HRH Prince Philip, when stationed on HMS Valiant *during World War II*

Clearer and colder preceded by light snow.

New York City's weather forecasters predicting the outlook
for March 12, 1888—the day of "The Blizzard of '88"

Well, I can tell you one thing, Blake—that song's got to go.

> *Marty Rackin, then Head of Production at Paramount, to Director*
> *Blake Edwards, about the song* Moon River *(by Henry Mancini*
> *and Johnny Mercer) in the 1961 movie* Breakfast at Tiffany's,
> *starring Audrey Hepburn. It scooped the Oscar for Best Song*

I cannot imagine anyone in their right mind leaving you for Camilla.

> *The Duke of Edinburgh in a 1996 letter to Diana, Princess of*
> *Wales, revealed in Paul Burrell's book* A Royal Duty

When anyone asks how I can best describe my experience in nearly 40 years at sea, I merely say, uneventful. Of course there have been winter gales, and storms and fog and the like but, in all my experience, I have never been in any accident of any sort worth speaking about... I never saw a wreck and never have been shipwrecked, nor was I ever in any predicament that threatened to end in disaster of any sort. You see, I am not very good material for a story.

> *Captain E. J. Smith, commander of the* Titanic, *in an*
> *interview before his ship's maiden voyage in 1912*

I'm staying on as leader. I've earned my right to be leader of this party. I'm sticking to that, I'm sticking to my job, and I will take this party into the next election.

> *Conservative leader Iain Duncan Smith's message to his shadow cabinet,*
> *October 2003. He was ousted by the end of the same month*

At 8.50 tonight, we shall be broadcasting Haydn's Cremation.

Announcer on BBC Radio 3

There will be no jobs or patronage—only decisions made on the merits.

Rudolph Giuliani, in June 1989—quoted in The New York Times
in June 1995, six years later, Raymond Harding, who supported
his failed 1989 campaign, found himself on the payroll

That rainbow song's no good. It slows the picture right down. Take it out.

Marty Rackin, then Head of Production at Paramount,
speaking of the song Over the Rainbow *(by Harold Arlen and E.Y.*
Harburg). It won the Oscar for Best Song. He was passing on Louis B.
Mayer's advice to cut out the whole Kansas scene, because it was "boring"

It just isn't believable.

Theater know-it-alls on hearing of actor Orson Welles' plan to
broadcast a dramatized account of H.G. Wells's story of alien invasion,
the War of the Worlds. *The radio broadcast created panic across the*
whole of the north east of the U. S., so convincing was Welles' broadcast

We've got to be careful, Ted—we don't want to go to a court of law with this.

Lord Archer, former deputy chairman of the Conservative
Party captured, allegedly on tape talking to his friend Ted Francis.
He wanted Ted to provide an alibi for him the night the
Daily Star *newspaper claimed that he, Archer, was with prostitute*
Monica Coghlan. But to court he went—and on to prison for perjury

It's time to get back to basics: to self-discipline and respect for the law, to consideration for others, to accepting responsibility for yourself and your family, and not shuffling it off on the State.

John Major, British Conservative Prime Minister from 1990 to 1997, speaking in 1993 as he launched the disastrous "Back to Basics" campaign, which promoted the virtue of family values. It transpired much later that Major had indeed been "back to basics" with MP Edwina Currie, in a four-year affair

What transformed an incident into a crisis was Nixon's endorsement of a cover-up, which began clumsily and continued stupidly.

Jonathan Aitken, disgraced Conservative cabinet minister, in his biography of President Richard Nixon—the words take on a fateful ring considering Aitken's own later career, which saw him in court on charges of perjury and perverting the course of justice

I think it is a shoddy, unusual thing to do to use the floor of the Senate to attack your opponent without any proof whatever.

Senator Joe McCarthy, finding the tables turned in 1956

Anyone who really knows me knows that I'm not a media hound and knows I'm trying to do the best within the situation I find myself.

Monica Lewinsky speaking in 2000—having already featured in a Jenny Craig diet program commercial (not to mention her Revlon contract and appearance hosting Saturday Night Live*)*

I called it a poof cloud... it developed and poof!—It was gone.

> *Dan McCarthy, forecaster, on the thunderstorm that later turned into*
> *an F5 tornado that tore through Oklahoma City on May 3, 1999, thereby*
> *demonstrating the unpredictability of weather and the importance of*
> *"ground truth" (i.e., eyewitnesses). "We don't really get to look out the*
> *window," said McCarthy. The storm had wind speeds of 318 mph,*
> *the fastest ever recorded. ("There are two cars in my yard," a City*
> *resident told a local paper, "and I have no idea who they belong to")*

A U. S. rapid response team is due to arrive in two weeks time with necessary equipment and expertise to determine the nature of the eruption.

> *Statement made two weeks* after *Mount Pago, a volcano in*
> *Papua New Guinea, had erupted in August 2002*

I've just grown up. I've totally changed everything in my life: my clothing, my men, everything.

> *Claudia Schiffer, supermodel—still working for l'Oréal, though.*
> The Observer, *"Quotes of the Week," July 8, 2001*

Now let's all try to settle this problem in a true Christian spirit.

> *Senator Warren Austin speaking at the United Nations*
> *in 1961, and referring to the Arab–Israeli crisis*

If excessive smoking actually plays a role in the production of lung cancer, it seems to be a minor one.

> *Dr. W. C. Heuper, of the National Cancer Institute,*
> *quoted in* The New York Times, *April 14, 1954*

For the majority of people, smoking has a beneficial effect.

> *Dr. Ian G. Macdonald, surgeon, quoted in* Newsweek, *November 18, 1963*

If we can't beat Paraguay we might as well go home.

> *Colin Montgomerie, Scottish captain of the golf team, before the*
> *1993 Alfred Dunhill Cup. They couldn't, and home they went*

It would be ridiculous for me to say I'm going to win but I'll be surprised and disappointed if I don't.

> *Johnny Miller, golf pro (later TV pundit), before the*
> *1974 U. S. Masters. He didn't finish in the top ten*

That's it. There's no way Ali can win this show.

> *Harry Carpenter, sports' commentator, during the*
> *famous "Rumble in the Jungle" boxing contest between*
> *George Foreman and Muhammad Ali in Zaïre (now*
> *Democratic Republic of the Congo) in 1973. Ali won*

When athletes in other sports lost whatever edge made them excel, they often
retired to a lifetime of golf. What, then, is Nicklaus to do?

> The Los Angeles Times *giving its verdict on golfer*
> *Jack Nicklaus, at the time of the 1986 US Masters*
> *championship. At the grand old age of 46, Nicklaus won it*

Well, if I can help you, I will. Don't worry about it.

> *Golfer Arnold Palmer to playing partner Billy Casper, in the 1966*
> *U. S. Open, who went on to win the title after Palmer collapsed*

I want to set women's lib back twenty years, to get women back in the home
where they belong. I will scrape her up. She is a woman and is subject to
women's emotional frailties. She will crack up during the match.

> *Bobby Riggs challenging Billie Jean King to a*
> *tennis match in 1973. She thrashed him (6–4, 6–3, 6–3)*

Britain's most fearless newspaper.

> *Slogan for the* Commonwealth Sentinel, *a newspaper launched*
> *by Mr. Lionel Burleigh in London in February, 1965. It lasted one*
> *day. Said Burleigh later, "We had forgotten to arrange any*
> *distribution...to my knowledge we only sold one copy"*

If Beethoven's Seventh Symphony is not by some means abridged, it will soon
fall into disuse.

> *Philip Hale, Boston music critic, writing in 1837*

I played over the music of that scoundrel Brahms. What a gift-less b*****d! It annoys me that this self-inflated mediocrity is hailed as a genius. Why, in comparison, Raff is a genius.

Tchaikovsky, writing in his diary in October 1886

You will never amount to very much.

Munich schoolmaster to young pupil by the name of Albert Einstein, aged ten

I can accept the theory of relativity as little as I can accept the existence of atoms and other such dogmas.

Ernst Mach (d. 1916), professor of physics at the University of Vienna

Night baseball is just a fad, a passing fancy.

*Phil Wrigley, American businessman
and president of Wrigley chewing gum*

We will no longer hang women up like pieces of meat.

*Larry Flynt—before the infamous and deliberately provocative Hustler
front cover showing a female body being pushed through a mincer*

If the wealth tax is going to be used to ease income tax at higher levels, then it must be a good thing for the future of the country and my children. I hope that the tax will change the pattern so that merit and hard work are rewarded at the expense of merely having.

*Sir Joseph, later Lord, Kagan, speaking in 1974. In 1980, Lord
Kagan was jailed for a string of offences, including tax evasion*

The Edsel is here to stay.

> *Henry Ford II, speaking in 1957 of the company's brand-new*
> *design (it lost the Ford Motor Company in excess of $250 million)*

A big world needs a very big bank.

> *Advertising slogan for commercial (starring Anthony Hopkins)*
> *for Barclays Bank, which the company was forced to ditch when*
> *news that the bank was to close 200 branches leaked out*

Few exercises exhilarate the financial world more than speculating what the Pennsylvania–New York Central Transportation Company will be doing in ten years' time if the great plans now being laid for the system come to fruition.

> Fortune Magazine *rejoicing at the merger of two railroad*
> *giants in 1965. In 1970 Penn Central went bust in what*
> *was then the biggest bankruptcy of all time ($4.6 billion)*

Phenomenally recession-proof.

> *John Gray, American head of "gentlemen's clubs" Spearmint Rhino.*
> *But in fall 2003, the London clubs, affected by layoffs and*
> *dwindling bonuses in the City's Square Mile, had yet to make a profit*

I know where the line is; I know how far I can go. My knowledge is great. I know what intimacies are. I know what secrets I keep safe...

> *Paul Burrell, interviewed on ABC news.*
> *"There are more?" asked the dumbfounded interviewer*

You aren't sexy enough.

> *Manager of New York's Copacabana Club to a*
> *female newcomer by the name of Goldie Hawn*

Whatever anyone says, I'm the one he comes home to, aren't I?

> *Dee Harrington on Rod Stewart, speaking in March*
> *1975—the year the singer met Britt Eckland*

We'll be together forever. We are like twins.

> *Britt Ekland, on her new love Rod Stewart, in 1976*

He falls instantly in and out of love. His present attachment will follow the
course of all the others.

> *Winston Churchill on the new (albeit uncrowned) King Edward*
> *VIII's liaison with American divorcée, Wallis Simpson, in 1936,*
> *which would lead to marriage and lifelong mutual adoration*

Biggs, it is my unpleasant duty to inform you that your earliest possible release
date is January 12, 1984.

> *Governor of Lincoln Jail, in the north of England,*
> *to a new inmate, train robber Ronald Biggs, in 1964*

I promise that truth shall be the policy of the Nixon–Agnew administration.

> *Spiro T. Agnew, Nixon's vice-president, speaking in 1968*

A third-rate burglary attempt not worthy of further White House comment.

Ron Ziegler, White House press spokesman
on the Watergate break-in, June 1972

I've got what it takes to stay.

Richard Nixon, November 1973

You're a man of the past. The future doesn't interest you.

French President Valéry Giscard d'Estaing, taunting his political
rival, François Mitterand, in a televized debate in 1973. Giscard
was the one later consigned to the dustbin, and Mitterand won in
1981—and went on to win two more presidential victories

Kate Graham's gonna get her tit caught in a big fat wringer if that's published!

U. S. Attorney General John Mitchell in September 1973, in a
phone interview with a Washington Post *journalist who was*
accusing him of running secret funds to finance covert intelligence
gathering. The article ran and Mitchell's career went down the pan

We have the momentum now, and I just know we are going to win.

President Gerald R. Ford, days before losing
the November 1976 election to Jimmy Carter

Our judgement is that the presence of the Royal Marines garrison...is sufficient deterrent against any possible aggressions.

> *Margaret Thatcher, predicting (incorrectly) that 48 marines*
> *would be sufficient to repel the entire Argentine military*

The spirit of victory is in the air!

> *Labour leader Hugh Gaitskell, before the party*
> *lost at the polls in the 1959 general election*

When I tell Dick Nixon what to do, he listens. I'm in charge.

> *John Mitchell, to Republican Congressmen in 1968*

I know I am going to be president.

> *Senator Gary Hart*

Constructive Republican Alternative Proposals.

> *The name of the committee set up by Gerald Ford,*
> *which came to be known by its pithier acronym CRAP*

We in America today are nearer the final triumph over poverty than anyone before in the history of the land...we have not yet reached the goal, but given a chance to go forward with the policies of the last eight years, we shall soon with the help of God be in the sight of the day when poverty will be banished from this nation.

> *President Herbert Hoover in 1928; the Wall Street Crash followed*
> *only a few months later, the start of the Great Depression*

You know, I always wondered about taping equipment, but I'm damn glad we
have it, aren't you?

> *Richard Nixon. In February, 2002, the Nixon Presidential*
> *Materials Staff released 500 more hours of taped conversations*
> *from the Nixon White House, bringing the total to 1,779 hours*
> *available in all. Though it wasn't the complete set*

I welcome this kind of examination, because people have got to know whether
or not their President is a crook. Well, I am not a crook.

> *Richard Nixon*

This is a discredited president.

> *Richard Nixon, speaking at the height of the Watergate affair, but he meant*
> *to say, "precedent." A Freudian slip if ever there was one*

You couldn't be elected dogcatcher.

> *Political pundit on the election fortunes of New York*
> *governor Nelson Rockefeller in 1966. The latter went*
> *on to win the election nobody thought he would*

Peace in our time.

> *Neville Chamberlain, British Prime Minister, returning from Munich*
> *with the famous "piece of paper" signed by Herr Hitler in 1938*

This is a hold up. Put all the money into a bag and hand it over.

> *One Eddie Blake, from Reno, Nevada, handing over a*
> *note with these words to a cashier in a bank in 1983 (written*
> *on the back of the envelope were his name and address)*

My God, this can't be true. They must mean the Philippines!

> *U. S. Secretary of the Navy, Frank Knox, when told that the*
> *Japanese had attacked Pearl Harbor, December 1941*

Don't worry. It's only Truman—you can't possibly lose.

> *Aides to Thomas A. Dewey, who was standing against*
> *Truman in the presidential election of 1948. Dewey*
> *was way ahead in the polls, but still got beaten*

Einstein has not a logical mind. Sometimes one feels like laughing. And
sometimes one feels a little irritated that such a hodgepodge can be seriously
accepted anywhere for thought.

> *The Very Reverend Jeremiah J. Callaghan,*
> *President of Duquesne University, Pittsburgh*

If they get anywhere, it will be without the vile-looking singer with the tyre-
tread lips.

> *TV producer on the first nationwide U. K. appearance of the*
> *Rolling Stones, fronted by lead singer Mick Jagger*

The war will be over by Christmas.

>*A phrase popular in 1861, during the American Civil War and it*
>*again enjoyed widespread currency at the start of World War I*

C'est une drôle de guerre.

>*The French Prime Minister, Edouard Daladier, on*
>*December 22, 1939; in the early days of World War II it*
>*seemed like nothing very much was happening. His phrase*
>*was translated as "a phony war" and became famous*

Whatever may be the reason—whether it was that Hitler thought he might get
away with what he had got without fighting for it, or whether it was that,
after all, the preparations were not sufficiently complete—however, one thing
is certain. He missed the bus.

>*Neville Chamberlain, British Prime Minister, speaking in April,*
>*1940 and referring to the apparent lack of activity by Nazi troops*

Let me say again. I don't believe in black majority rule ever in Rhodesia. Not in a
thousand years.

>*Ian Smith, speaking in 1976 while still ruler of Rhodesia (now*
>*Zimbabwe). Black majority rule became a reality in 1979*

And now before us stands the last problem that must be solved and will be solved. It is the last territorial claim which I have to make in Europe, but it is the claim from which I will not recede.

> *Adolf Hitler on September 26, 1938, speaking at the Berlin*
> *Sportpalast—prior to his invasion of Czechoslovakia and*
> *annexation of the German-speaking Sudetenland*

Let the Nazis come on. We are not afraid.

> *Dr. Engelbert Dollfuss, Austrian Chancellor, speaking in February 1934*

We see ourselves as a true white State in Southern Africa, with a possibility of granting a full future to the black man in our midst.

> *Dr. Hendrik Verwoerd, February 1960*

The case is a loser.

> *Johnnie Cochran on the prospects of winning the O. J. Simpson*
> *murder trial, July 1994. Simpson won*

Well, don't worry about it.

> *Lieutenant Kermit Tyler, duty officer, hearing that blips had been picked*
> *up by a radar operator on Oahu Island—the blips were aircraft carriers of*
> *the Japanese fleet, from which the aircraft bound for Pearl Harbor,*
> *Hawaii, were launched on December 7, 1941. From* Snatching Defeat
> from the Jaws of Victory, *by David Wragg (Sutton Publishing, 2000)*

Let us understand, North Vietnam cannot defeat or humiliate the United States.
Only Americans can do that.

Richard Nixon, 1969

We should declare war on North Vietnam... We could pave the whole country
and put parking strips on it, and still be home by Christmas.

Ronald Reagan, 1965

Iraq will triumph and with Iraq our Arab nation and mankind also triumph.

Saddam Hussein, on Iraqi television three hours
after the air strikes of the 2003 Gulf War began

Q: Mr. Secretary, what evidence do you have that it's actually working, that
there are actually Iraqis who are heeding this call to—
Rumsfeld: We have evidence.
Q: And what sort of evidence is that?
Rumsfeld: Good evidence.

News briefing from Secretary Rumsfeld
and General Myers, March 20, 2003

My only fear is that the Zulu will not fight.

Lieutenant Lord Chelmsford, commander of British
forces at Rorke's Drift, before the invasion of Zululand.
The Zulus proved to be formidable warriors

We are going to find a solution to the Middle East conflict as soon as the Arabs agree with us.

Moshe Dayan, Israeli Minister of Defense during the Six Day War in 1967

The Ruhr will not be subject to a single bomb. If an enemy bomber reaches the Ruhr, my name is not Herman Goering—you can call me Meier.

Herman Goering, Head of the Luftwaffe, in
August 9, 1939—before bombing of the Ruhr began

All you have to do is go down to the bottom of your swimming pool and hold your breath.

David Miller, U. S. Department of Environment spokesman, on how
to protect yourself from radiation caused by a nuclear explosion

Exhilaration and lasting euphoria, which in no way differs from the normal euphoria of the healthy person... You perceive an increase in self-control and possess more vitality and capacity for work. In other words, you are simply more normal, and it is soon hard to believe that you are under the influence of any drug.

Sigmund Freud, the father of psychoanalysis, writing in 1884 about cocaine

Distival can be given with complete safety to pregnant women and nursing mothers without adverse effect on mother or child.

Reassuring notice on a drug advertisement in the British Medical Journal
in 1960. Unfortunately the drug went by another name—thalidomide

The Libyan army is capable of destroying America and breaking its nose.

General Gaddafi

New Leadership in '88: Dukakis–Jackson.

Slogan on button during the U. S. presidential campaign
in 1988, when Jesse Jackson ran with Michael Dukakis

Intelligence gathered by this and other governments leaves no doubt that the
Iraq regime continues to possess and conceal some of the most lethal
weapons ever devised.

President George W. Bush, speaking in his March 2003 address
to the nation. Two years earlier (in February 2001), Secretary of
State Colin Powell, on a trip to Egypt, had said "He (Saddam
Hussein) has not developed any significant capability with
respect to weapons of mass destruction. He is unable to
project conventional power against his neighbors"

I've been married to this man for 26 years and I can tell you one thing—he's not a
homosexual, or is he bisexual. He's a wonderful, loving husband.

Tammy Faye Bakker, on Nightline, *May 27, 1987. An*
article later appeared in Penthouse entitled "The Devil
in Jim Bakker: His Homosexual Lover and Pimp Tells All"

God sent me there to bring an abrupt end to the immorality and financial fraud
   of this "religious soap opera" that had become an international
   embarrassment to the Christian gospel.

> *Televangelist Jim Bakker, describing his stint as head of
> the TV show* Praise The Lord—*following which he was
> convicted of embezzlement to the tune of $3.7 million and
> sentenced to 45 years in prison (he served less than five years)*

Follow me around. I don't care. I'm serious. If anybody wants to put a tail on me,
   go ahead. They'd be very bored.

> *Gary Hart, U. S. senator and frontrunner for the Democratic Presidential
> nomination in 1987, when he was carrying on with Donna Rice*

The Army is the Indian's best friend.

> *General George Armstrong Custer, Civil War commander who died
> in the Battle of the Little Big Horn against the Sioux and Cheyenne
> Indians. The words were uttered six years before that battle in 1870*

Has there ever been danger of war between Germany and ourselves, members
   of the same Teutonic race? Never has it been imagined.

> *Andrew Carnegie, Scottish-born U. S. entrepreneur,
> in* The Baseless Fear of War *(1913)*

That virus is a pussycat.

> *Dr. Peter Duesberg (Professor of Molecular Biology at the University of*
> *California at Berkeley), referring to HIV, in the* Journal of the American
> Association for the Advancement of Science, *March 25, 1988*

The AIDS virus is roughly 450 times smaller than the spermatozoon. The
spermatozoon can easily pass through the "net" that is formed by the
condom. These margins of uncertainty should represent an obligation on the
part of the health ministries and all these campaigns to act in the same way
as they do with regard to cigarettes, which they state to be a danger.

> *Cardinal Alfonso Lopez Trujillo, president of the Vatican's*
> *Pontifical Council for the Family, on BBC's* Panorama *program,*
> *playing down the condom's role in stopping the spread of AIDS*

I laughed... till my sides were sore.

> *Adam Sedgwick, British geologist, describing,*
> *in a letter to Charles Darwin, his reaction to reading*
> *the latter's* opus magnum, The Origin of Species, *1859*

I think that the sooner people emancipate themselves from this false worship of
Shakespeare the better it will be—first because people when they are freed
from this falsehood will come to understand that a drama which has no
religious basis is not only not an important or a good thing, as is now
supposed, but is a most trivial and contemptible affair.

> *Tolstoy, writing about the plays of William Shakespeare*

An interesting tour-de-force, though not up to the level of the author's two previous novels.

> The New York Times Book Review *on Anthony Burgess's 1963 novel* A Clockwork Orange *(the two previous novels are titles few can recall)*

What is to stop a woman who is interested in national and international affairs from reading magazines that deal with those subjects?

> The New York Times Book Review *on* The Feminine Mystique *by Betty Friedan in 1963 (a key work in formulating feminist thought) accusing it of "sweeping generalities"*

It fails... because half its incidents are farcical and fantastic.

> The New York Times Book Review *on* Catch-22 *by Joseph Heller in 1961*

This sort of thing may be tolerated by the French, but we are British— thank God.

> *Viscount Montgomery, British military leader, on the Homosexuality Bill being presented in parliament in 1965*

The Congress will push me to raise taxes, and I'll say no. And they'll push, and I'll say no. And they'll push again, and I'll say to them: "Read my lips—no new taxes"

> *George H. W. Bush in 1988, when he was nominated to run for president. The phrase came back to haunt him when subsequently he had to raise tax*

We're through the looking glass here people.

Jim Garrison (The New Orleans District Attorney
who was among the first to theorize that the J. F. K.
assassination was the result of a conspiracy)

You side with your brother against your cousin, and with your cousin against
the foreigners.

Old Arab saying. (A saying that many Western politicians tend to forget)

I bet it's a pip!

Bette Davis, turning down the part of Scarlett O'Hara in the
American Civil War epic Gone With the Wind, in 1938

Don't be a damn fool, David. This picture is going to be one of the biggest white
elephants of all time.

Comment by Victor Fleming to David O. Selznick, who'd
offered the director a percentage of cinema receipts instead
of a salary for directing the movie Gone With the Wind

Kinnock will be prime minister.

Tony Benn speculating in his diaries on the outcome of the 1992
general election in the U.K. Kinnock lost to John Major

Wow, this is really incredible, we finished the movie, it's in the can, fantastic—
and everybody got hurt except me. Ha, ha, ha!

> *Tobe Hooper, director of the 1974 horror movie*
> The Texas Chain Saw Massacre *(during which everyone—but*
> *everyone—got hurt) before the porch on which he was sitting*
> *collapsed, resulting in him being stabbed by six-inch nails*

[I'd] never dream of selling Diana's letters.

> *James Hewitt, former lover of the late Diana, Princess of Wales,*
> *speaking (in a statement issued through his solicitor) in April 1998.*
> *Fast forward to January 2003, when the ex-Life Guards army officer*
> *declared: "I think it might be irresponsible not to sell them." In December*
> *2002 he was exposed trying to sell them for £10 million by a reporter*

Talking pictures are a very interesting invention, but I do not believe that they
will remain long in fashion. First of all, perfect synchronization between
sound and image is absolutely impossible, and, secondly, cinema cannot, and
must not, become theater.

> *Jean-Louis Lumiere, French inventor, quoted in* Films Sonores Avant, *1928*

I'd probably say foolish things.

> *President George W. Bush, when he was asked*
> *what would happen if he had an alcoholic drink today.*
> *Reported in* The Washington Post, *July 25, 1999*

You know I could run for governor, but I'm basically a media creation. I've never done anything. I've worked for my dad. I worked in the oil business. But that's not the kind of profile you have to have to get elected to public office.

President George W. Bush, speaking back in 1989

The War that will End War

Title of a book by H. G. Wells that was published in 1914 on the eve of World War I. It was a phrase the writer would live to rue

We must let a hundred flowers bloom.

The slogan for what would turn out to be a short-lived period of permissible free expression in Chairman Mao's China, first mooted in 1956 and as a result of which hundreds of intellectual leaders were executed

Supposing one submarine pops up opposite the town of Gallipoli and waves a Union Jack three times, the whole Turkish garrison on the peninsula will take to their heels and make a bee line for Bulair.

Lord Kitchener assuring General Sir Ian Hamilton that the Turkish defenses at Gallipoli (where British and Australian troops landed on April 25, 1915) might be brought to its knees with a single British submarine in the Sea of Marmara, Turkey. From Damn the Dardanelles! The Story of Gallipoli *by John Laffin (Osprey, 1980)*

However much we may sympathize with a small nation confronted by a big and powerful neighbor, we cannot in all circumstances undertake to involve the whole British Empire in a war simply on her account. If we have to fight it must be on larger issues than that...

Neville Chamberlain, after Hitler's Nazi armies had invaded the Sudetenland

Germany is prepared to agree to any solemn pact of non-aggression, because she does not think of attacking but only of acquiring security.

Adolf Hitler, 1933

This year will go down in history. For the first time, a civilized nation has full gun registration! Our streets will be safer, our police more efficient, and the world will follow our lead into the future!

Adolf Hitler, on the passing of the German Weapons Act in 1935

The German people are not a warlike nation. It is a soldierly one, which means it does not want a war, but does not fear it. It loves peace but also loves its honor and freedom.

Adolf Hilter

England, unlike in 1914, will not allow herself to blunder into a war lasting for years... Such is the fate of rich countries. Not even England has the money nowadays to fight a world war. What should England fight for? You don't get yourself killed over an ally.

Adolf Hitler, 1939

The Berlin–Rome–Tokyo alliance [i.e. Nazi Germany, Fascist Italy, and Imperial Japan] is a worldwide spiritual program of the young peoples of the world. It is defeating the international alliance of convenience of Anglo-Saxon imperialist monopolists and unlimited Bolshevist internationalism. It is showing the world the way to a better future.

Albrecht Fürst von Urach

The League of Nations is still strong enough by its collective actions to avert or arrest aggression... There is no room for bargaining or compromise.

Foreign commissar Litvinoff, September 21, 1938. The League of Nations had been set up by treaty after World War I amid high hopes that it would prevent future wars

Millions now living will never die!

Judge Rutherford, American spiritualist, to a packed Albert Hall in London during the 1920s

Here comes Jonny Wilkinson... Mr One Hundred Per Cent.

ITV commentator on the England–Samoa rugby union World Cup match, October 26, 2003—seconds before the England fly half missed a kick at goal, leaving the crowd gasping in astonishment

WE LOVE YOU VERY MUCH + MOM IS DEAD

Telegram conveying "birthday greetings" sent by Western Union in 1983. It should have read WE LOVE YOU VERY MUCH + MOM AND DAD; it didn't, and the company was sued for the emotional trauma caused

We are puzzling our heads as how best to make use of them and have not yet come to a decision. They are not going to take the British Army straight to Berlin as some people imagine, but if properly used and skilfully handled by the detachments who work them they may be very useful in taking trenches and strong points. Some people are rather too optimistic as to what these weapons will accomplish.

> *Deputy of the General (later Field Marshal Lord) Sir Douglas Haig writing about the tank, a new weapon of war, in 1916. From* The Western Front *by Richard Holmes (BBC Books, 1999)*

The Misappliance of
Science—20/20 Visionaries

There will be no epidemics. There will be no incurable diseases. Medical and
surgical treatment will reduce crime to a fraction of its present-day
proportion.

> *Norman Bel Geddes, "Ten Years From Now,"*
> Ladies Home Journal, *1931*

There is no danger the *Titanic* will sink. The boat is unsinkable and nothing but
inconvenience will be suffered by the passengers.

> *Phillip Franklin, vice-president of the White Star Line*

Man will never reach the moon regardless of all future scientific advances.

> *Dr. Lee De Forest, inventor of the vacuum tube and father of television*

All people born after the year 2000 will, barring accidents, live indefinitely.

> *Arthur C. Clarke, 1962*

Euthanasia of the weak and sensual is possible and I have little doubt that it will be planned and achieved. The men of the new republic will not be squeamish in inflicting death—killing will be done with an opiate. The next hundred years will see a process of physical and mental improvement in mankind.

> *The British novelist H. G. Wells, writing in 1900 in* Anticipations *and sounding an ominous alarm, though it has to be said we didn't get his Invisible Man, a Time Machine, or a War of The Worlds with invading Martians either*

Long before the 1990s, America will have no very rich or very poor. And the family will be restricted to the capacity of the parents to maintain and educate it.

> *T.V. Powderly, 1893*

Railways can be of no advantage to rural areas, since agricultural products are too heavy or too voluminous to be transported by them.

> *F. J. B. Noel, from a pamphlet (1842) entitled* The Railroads will be Ruinous for France and Especially for the Cities Through Which They Go

I find it difficult to believe that the seat belt can afford the driver any great amount of protection over and above that which is available to him through the medium of the safety-type steering wheel if he has his hands on the wheel and grips the rim sufficiently tight to take advantage of its energy-absorption properties and also takes advantage of the shock-absorbing action which can be achieved by correct positioning of the feet and legs.

> *General Motors vehicle safety engineer Howard Gandelot in 1954*

California, 1984: to those of us who remember the hurricanes of the 1960s, with their grimly girlish names and their incredible viciousness, a certain excitement has gone out of life. It turned out that hurricanes could be prevented rather easily.

Dr. Roger Revelle, New Scientist, *1964*

Despite the trend to compactness and lower costs, it is unlikely everyone will have his own computer any time soon.

Stanley Penn of the Wall Street Journal, *1966*

Nobody who is anybody a hundred years hence but will have his automobile and his air yacht.

The Brooklyn Daily Eagle, *December 30, 1900, in an article entitled "Things will be so different 100 years hence"*

A familiar old gadget which has been around for hundreds of years is just about to get pensioned off forever—the key! By the mid-1980s no-one will ever need to hide a key under the doormat again.

Computer scientist Christopher Evans, The Micro Millennium, *1979*

That fellow Charles Lindbergh will never make it. He's doomed.

Harry Guggenheim, aviation enthusiast

Computers will benefit even more than telephones from the development of integrated circuits in ever smaller "chips," and very small computers may emerge. Most computers will probably still occupy a large room, however, because of the space needed for the ancillary software—the tapes and cards to be fed in, the operating staff, and the huge piles of paper for printing out the results. But future computers, though no smaller, will be capable of doing far more than their predecessors.

Professor Desmond King-Hele, The End of the Twentieth Century, *1970*

Your clothing will be informal, lightweight, easily adaptable to changes in climate (in 1982). Even men will lean to bright and comfortable apparel in the office. Some clothing will be made of paper products and priced so low that you will be able to dispose of it after a couple of wearings.

Changing Times Magazine, *1957*

It may, however, be safe to assume that it will hardly be possible to apply electricity to haul great passenger trains.

George H. Daniels, railroad executive, Brooklyn Daily Eagle, *1900*

No flying machine will ever fly from New York to Paris.

Orville Wright, 1908

In the year 2000, virtue never goes unrewarded!

Line from a play by French author Nicolas-Edme Restif de la Bretonne, entitled The Year 2000, *which he wrote in 1789. In his vision of the future, there are no lawyers and a fair and virtuous king rules society. We all share at least 50% of his vision*

By the year 2000, housewives will probably have a robot "maid" shaped like a
box with one large eye on the top, several arms and hands, and long narrow
pads on the side for moving about.

New York Times, *1966*

With the first moon colonies predicted for the 70s, preliminary work is moving
ahead on the types of shelter that will be required to maintain men on the moon.

Arnold B. Barach and the Kiplinger Washington
Editors, 1975 and the Changes to Come, *1962*

Comets are not heavenly bodies, but originate in the earth's atmosphere below
the moon.

Augustion de Angelis of the Clementine College, Rome, 1673

Drinking in excess is plainly on the decrease. And with every step in this
direction, the self-respect of the people must grow, pauperism decrease, and
an enlightened conception of public duty develop. Whatever else the
twentieth century brings about, we may reasonably look for a great
revolution in the political status of the world.

Charles Morris, The Marvelous Record of the Closing Century, *1899*

Within a few years, he [Dr. Edward Warner, President of the Council of the
International Civil Aviation Organization] said, there will be nothing to
prevent a five-hundred passenger plane being built but there will be no
economic advantage to constructing one.

The New York Times *reports on a forthcoming*

UN radio broadcast dedicated to the International
Civil Aviation Organization, April 23, 1950

It is hardly necessary to inform you that life in those times will be as nearly a
holiday as it is possible to make it. Work will be reduced to a minimum by
machinery.

The Brooklyn Daily Eagle, *December 30, 1900, in an article*
entitled "Things will be so different 100 years hence"

In this city, smoke will be eliminated, noise will be conquered, and impurity will
be eliminated from the air.

From "Cities of Tomorrow," a feature in
Amazing Stories *by Julian Krupa, 1939*

[The flying tank] will be a greater guarantee of peace than all the treaties that
human ingenuity can concoct.

J. Walter Christie on his invention which he described as "the
most revolutionary war invention since the discovery of
gunpowder," in the July 1932 issue of Modern Mechanics *(the*
strap on the front cover was "Flying tanks shed wings")

[Electricity in the future will be] too cheap to meter...

Thus wrote Charles Steinmetz, Chief Engineer for General Electric, in an article
entitled "You will think this is a dream" for Ladies Home Journal *in 1915*

From every point of view, therefore, except perhaps that of the exceptional woman who would be able to hold her own against masculine competition—and men always issue informal letters of naturalization to such an exceptional woman—the woman suffrage which leads up to feminism would be a social disaster.

Sir Almroth E. Wright, in The Unexpurgated Case Against Woman Suffrage, *1913*

The Queen is most anxious to enlist everyone who can speak or write to join in checking this mad wicked folly of "woman's rights," with all its attendant horrors, on which her poor sex is bent, forgetting every sense of womanly feeling and propriety. God created men and women different—then let them remain each in their own position. Woman would become the most hateful, heartless, and disgusting of human beings were she allowed to unsex herself; and where would be the protection which man was intended to give the weaker sex?

Queen Victoria, in a letter dated 1870. The head of a vast British Empire that then covered much of the globe clearly considered herself an exception to the rule

The peculiar horror of her book—*Wise Parenthood*—is that it is couched in pseudo-scientific terms, and is addressed to the married woman.

Newspaper review of the book written by Marie Stopes (author of the million-selling Married Love*) which, published in 1918, was the first to tackle the subject of family planning. Equally outraged, the* News *of the World offered a free willow-pattern*

tea tray as a gift to all mothers of ten children. Doctors claimed
that women who used contraception were apt to become
"prurient, foul-mouthed and foul-minded with advancing years"

Heaven and Earth were created all together in the same instant, on October
23rd, 4004 BC at nine o'clock in the morning.

Dr. John Lightfoot, vice-chancellor of Cambridge University
England, before the publication of Darwin's The Origin of Species

Cannabis indica is one of the best additions to cough mixtures that we possess,
as it quiets the tickling in the throat, and yet does not constipate or depress
the system as does morphine.

Hobart Hare in Practical Therapeutics, 1895

Animals, which move, have limbs and muscles. The Earth does not possess
limbs and muscles; therefore it does not move.

Scipio Chiaramonti, Professor of Philosophy and
Mathematics at the University of Pisa, Italy, in 1633

I have always consistently opposed high-tension and alternating systems of
electric lighting (AC current)... not only on account of danger but because of
their general unreliability and unsuitability for any general system of
distribution.

Thomas Edison, "The Dangers of Electric Lighting" in
the North American Review, November 1889

The actual building of roads devoted to motor cars is not for the near future, in
spite of many rumors to that effect.

Harpers Weekly, *August 2, 1902*

[Ford] is nothing but an assemblage plant.

Frederic L. Smith, President of the Association of Licensed
Automobile Manufacturers (A. L. A. M.). In 1903 Henry Ford had
lodged a request for the Ford Motor Company to join the association

We hope that Professor Langley will not put his substantial greatness as a
scientist in further peril by continuing to waste his time and the money
involved, in further airship experiments. Life is short, and he is capable of
services to humanity incomparably greater than can be expected to result
from trying to fly... For students and investigators of the Langley type there
are more useful employments.

The New York Times *commenting on the*
American aviation pioneer Samuel Langley

Housekeeping which a hundred years ago was regarded as drudgery is now
fun—a real joyful picnic.

The Knoxville Journal *of 1900, looking ahead in an*
article entitled "The Progress of Science in 2000"

How fortunate we are to be living on this first day of the twentieth century! Let
us make a wish that as the nineteenth century vanishes into the abyss of
time, it takes away all the idiotic hatreds and recriminations that have

saddened our days, which are unworthy of the twentieth-century Frenchman. Have a good century!

Article in the French newspaper Le Figaro, *January 1, 1901*

Machinery will be doing all the unpleasant work while humanity will be making beautiful things or reading books.

Oscar Wilde, in The Spirit of Man under Socialism, *1891*

The century that left us yesterday had numerous glories: steam engines, electricity, steam boats, antiseptics, anaesthetics. The coming century only has to continue such glories to achieve greatness.

Le Figaro *newspaper, January 1, 1901*

It is not at all probable that the model newspaper of the new century will exceed ten or 12 pages.

Ernest F. Birmingham, editor and publisher of the now defunct Fourth Estate newspaper group, speculating in the early 1900s on the future of newspaper publishing. He concluded his article with the following comment: "careful observers of matters journalistic have expressed their opinion that the prodigal use of pictures that now marks the most popular of the penny newspapers [viz. those of William Randolph Hearst and Joseph Pulitzer] has become such a nuisance that a reaction is certain to follow in the near future"

Control your Irish passions, Thomas. Your uncle here tells me you proposed 64
    lifeboats and he had to pull your arm to get you down to 32. Now, I will
    remind you just as I reminded him: these are my ships. And, according to our
    contract, I have final say on the design. I'll not have so many little boats, as
    you call them, cluttering up my decks and putting fear into my passengers.

> *J. Bruce Ismay, director of the White Star Line,*
> *to Thomas Andrews, managing director of Harland*
> *and Wolff Shipyards, where the* Titanic *was built*

By 1980 all power (electric, atomic, solar) is likely to be virtually costless.

> *Henry Luce, American media mogul, back in 1956*

In fifteen years, more electricity will be sold for electric vehicles than for light.

> *Thomas Edison, American inventor, speaking in 1910*

There is no likelihood that man can ever tap the power of the atom.

> *Dr Robert Millikan, 1923*

Atomic energy might be as good as our present-day explosives but it is unlikely
    to produce anything very much more dangerous.

> *Winston Churchill, 1939*

We shall never get people whose time is money to take much interest in atoms.

> *Samuel Butler*

The horse-less carriage is a luxury for the wealthy. It will never, of course, come into such common use as the bicycle.

The Literary Digest, *in 1889*

Tell the Vietnamese they've got to draw in their horns or we're going to bomb them back into the Stone Age.

General Curtis LeMay, May 1964

Airplanes can barely keep themselves in the air. How can they carry any kind of load?

William Pickering, astronomer, in 1908

Airplanes suffer from so many technical faults that it is only a matter of time before any reasonable man realizes they are useless.

Scientific American *(1910)*

To throw bombs from an airplane will do as much damage as throwing bags of flour. It will be my pleasure to stand on the bridge of any ship while it is attacked by airplanes.

Newton Barker, U. S. Minister of Defense, 1921

The only thing that will happen is that the vessel will sink, and suffocate the crew.

H. G. Wells, writing about the submarine in 1902—
they had been in use since around 1850

Even if a submarine should work by miracle, it will never be used. No country in
the world would use such a vicious and petty form of warfare.

William Henderson, British Admiral, in 1914

Samuel Morse must have lost his mind if he believes in this idea himself.

*Senator Oliver Hampton Smith, having witnessed a
demonstration of Morse's recent invention in 1842*

It is only righteous that Joshua Coppersmiths, who has tried to find investors to
finance the development of a so-called telephone, is arrested for fraud.

Article in the Boston Post *(1865)*

Use your time on something useful. All the radios this country will ever need
can easily fit on my desk.

*W. W. Dean, director of the American phone company W. W.
Dean, in 1907, to Lee De Forrest, one of the early radio pioneers*

Radio is just a fashion contrivance that will soon die out. It is obvious that there
will never be invented a proper receiver.

Thomas Edison, American inventor

You're intending to make a ship sail against wind and tide by lighting a fire
below deck? I don't have time to listen to that kind of nonsense.

*The French Emperor Napoleon, on the inventor
Robert Fulton's plans to design a steamboat*

The Patent Galvanic Rings And Christie's Magnetic Fluid

This remarkable discovery has received the universal approbation of the
medical professional of Europe. Who have pronounced it among the most
important of modern scientific inventions.

1844 newspaper advertisement for above product;
part of the vogue for magnetic medicines

A certain proportion of at least the most militant suffragists are neurotics who
in some instances are compensating for masculine trends, in others, are more
or less successfully sublimating sadistic and homosexual ones.

H. W. Frink writing on the early feminists in 1918

Nuclear-powered vacuum cleaners will probably be a reality within ten years.

Alex Lewyt, U. S. inventor, quoted in the New York Times *in 1955*

This fool wishes to reverse the entire science of astronomy.

Martin Luther, architect of the Protestant Reformation in
Continental Europe, speaking of Copernicus in about 1543

The talking motion picture will not supplant the regular motion picture... There
is such tremendous investment in pantomime pictures that it would be
absurd to disturb it.

Thomas Edison (attributed), American inventor, in 1913

It's the End of the World as We Know It

At 7 a.m. on "X Day" the men from Planet X, or XISTS, will arrive on Earth, close a deal with "Bob," leader and "High Epopt" of the Church of the SubGenius, rapture the card-carrying Ordained SubGenii up to the Escape Vessels of the Sex Goddesses, and destroy the remaining population on Earth.

Prediction by the Church of the SubGenius for the end of the world—all well and good, except it was to have taken place on July 5, 1998

End of the world on May 18!

Caption on apocalyptic postcards being sold on streets in Germany in early 1910; many believed the imminent arrival of Halley's Comet signaled that the end of the world was nigh. It was even thought that cyanide gas from the comet's tail would extinguish humankind, and street quacks plied "comet pills" as antidotes

We may have another year, maybe two years. Then I believe it is going to
be over.

> *A young Billy Graham speaking in 1950, quoted by Hugo McCord in a 1997*
> *article published online at Bible-Infonet. (Graham later revised the date,*
> *wrote McCord, saying instead that 1998 would be the year)*

88 Reasons Why Christ Will Come Back in 1988.

> *Title of a book by self-styled prophet*
> *Harold Whisenant, clearly missing the word "not"*

Sometime between April 16 and 23, 1957, Armageddon will sweep the world!
Millions of persons will perish in its flames and the land will be scorched.

> Watchtower *magazine*

Our planet is on collision course with something we don't even have a word for.

> *Terence McKenna. The 1990s psychedelic guru didn't stick*
> *around to find out. He died of cancer three years later*

It said "Tzaruch shemirah" and "Hasof bah"... which essentially means that
everyone needs to account for themselves because the end is near.

> *Zalman Rosen, one of a small crowd to have witnessed*
> *the mystical visitation by a 20lb carp that started shouting*
> *(in Hebrew) at the fish market in New Square, New York*
> *state, January 2003. Said his co-worker Luis Nivelo, "I don't*
> *believe any of this Jewish stuff, but I heard that fish talk"*

If Christ does not appear to meet his 144,000 faithful shortly after midnight on February 6th or 7th, it means that my calculations, based on the Bible, must be revised.

> *Mrs Margaret Rowan, a Californian harbinger*
> *of doom, to her group the Advanced Adventists. The*
> *said evening of February 6, 1925, passed uneventfully*

The Earth is degenerating these days. Bribery and corruption abound. Children no longer mind their parents, every man wants to write a book, and it is evident that the end of the world is fast approaching.

> *Assyrian Stone Tablet, c. 2800 B. C.*

Dear Friends... This world is in haste and is drawing ever closer to its end, and it always happens that the longer it lasts, the worse it becomes. And so it must ever be, for the coming of the Anti-Christ grows ever more evil because of the sins of the people, and then truly it will be grim and terrible widely in the world.

> *Archbishop Wulfstan of York, in his famous*
> Sermon of the Wolf to the English, *(opening paragraph,*
> *translated by Dr Andy Orchard), which he wrote down in 1014*
> *when millennial fears were reaching a frenzied peak*

The world will end with a giant flood on February 20, 1524.

> *Johannes Stoeffler, a German astrologer who shot to fame in the sixteenth*
> *century because of his "great" if not entirely accurate predictions*

The world will be destroyed by fire on April 3, 1843.

> *William Alexander Miller, hugely popular harbinger of doom in*
> *the U. S. in the 1830s. He attracted an enormous following, and*
> *his predictions even appeared in the* New York Herald. *April 3 came*
> *and went without incident, and Miller lived to the age of 67, dying in 1849*

The end is nigh; mile-wide asteroid is due to destroy human race at 6.30 p.m. on October 26, 2028.

> *Headline in the* Scottish Daily Record *on March 13, 1998. Watch this space*

Acknowledgments

The author would like to thank the staff at the London Library and at the British Library, where this book was researched and written—and fellow readers at the latter institution, for their moral support.

Deciding who should be 'in' and who would be left out was a difficult task, and I make no apologies for the fact that this book is, of necessity, a personal and highly eclectic selection. Many, many works and volumes, too numerous to list, were consulted—some proved to be rich sources of background information, while others were of doubtful veracity. An early classic of the genre to which a nod is certainly due is the *Last Words of Famous Men* by the pseudonymous Bega, published in London in 1930 and on which so many later works have drawn for material. Also to be acknowledged are the many early recorders of tombstone inscriptions and epitaphs, many of which would now be lost to the elements had it not been for their strange enthusiasms and careful jottings.

Last, but not least, a word of thanks is also due to my splendid husband for all his support—and for creating so many wonderful meals to keep body and soul together during the writing of this book.